Success
Is Just
One Wish
Away

Other books by Jon Spoelstra

Ice to the Eskimos: How to Sell a Product Nobody Wants
How to Sell the Last Seat in the House
Your Profits Are Brought to You by . . .

Jon Spoelstra

Success Is Just One Wish Away

*Make Just One Wish and
Your Life Suddenly Changes.*

*But Make Sure
It's the Right One.*

DELSTAR™

Success Is Just One Wish Away may be purchased for personal, educa-
tional, or business use. For quantity purchases, please note discount
schedule on last page of book.

First Edition

Cover Design: Ron Hughes

Spoelstra, Jon.
    Success is just one wish away : make just one wish and your
    life suddenly changes : but make sure it's the right one
    / Jon Spoelstra.—1st ed.
        p. cm.
        ISBN: 1-891686-15-1
        1. Wishes—Fiction. 2. Success in business—Fiction.
    3. Motivation (Psychology)—Fiction. I. Title.

PS3569.P62O64   1998   813'54
                        QBI98-669

98 99 00 01 DSB 10 9 8 7 6 5 4 3 2 1

DelStar Books
3350 Palms Center Drive
Las Vegas, NV 89103
Phone: (702) 798-9000
Fax: (702) 597-2002

"Half the failures in life arise from pulling in one's horse as he is leaping."

—Julius Hare (1795–1855) and
Augustus Hare (1792–1834),
English clerics and writers
(*Guesses at Truth,* Series #1, 1827)

This book is dedicated to those readers who choose to jump on the right horse—and you will find out which horse is the right one in this book—and ride, *ride like the wind.*

Chapter 1

This is the most unusual—maybe even wacky—story that you have ever heard. Ever.

Even though you may disbelieve parts of it or even lots of it, I ask you just one favor. Suspend your disbelief for just a little while.

Go ahead, pretend you're a kid again and put your disbelief to rest. If you do, this story will have a profound effect on you. How so? In a nutshell, your life might never again be the same.

My story starts simply enough. It starts with an aerosol can. On an Oregon beach.

The beaches in Oregon are the best walking beaches in the world. When it's low tide, the water recedes up to a hundred yards, leaving hard-packed sand. If you wanted to string up a net, the surface would be tournament-ready for playing tennis. When you walk close to the waves, you can find all kinds of neat shells just lying there on the hard sand. Like sand dollars. And, occasionally, a Chinaman's cap, a small shell that does look like . . . well . . . a China-man's cap.

In the winter, you can walk for miles and not see anybody. The weather's not bad— usually in the fifties—and the scenery is terrific with huge rock outcroppings, forests and the blustery sea. If you ever wanted to just walk and think, think and walk, this is the place.

Walking with my head down scanning the sand, I saw an aerosol can. There's not a lot of litter on the beach—I think the ocean sort of sucks that stuff up and somehow distributes it to the New Jersey shore or someplace like that—so seeing the can was unusual. Even more unusual were the words on it. They were in Japanese.

This wasn't your normal litter. This had to have floated the seven thousand miles from Japan!

I picked it up. As I said, the copy on the can was in Japanese. I couldn't read a thing. But it looked like an aerosol can of paint. I couldn't tell what color. I decided to give it a try to see if the color was blue or maybe some exotic fluorescent color.

I pressed the nozzle.

Nothing happened.

I pressed again. Nothing.

Then I felt movement inside the can. It felt like a frog thrashing to get out. Whirling and bumping and jumping. Just as I was going to drop the can on the sand, an explosion of smoke and mist fired out of the nozzle. That's when I first met my genie.

From that point on, my life changed more than you could imagine. This is the first time I've ever told anybody about this. After all, I didn't want to be labeled as some crazy like those people that claim they were abducted by UFOs or those people that claim they've seen Bigfoot.

UFOs can be explained, I think. The same for Bigfoot. *But a genie in an aerosol can?* No way! That's so off the wall it would be too bizarre even for the tabloids. And it is so outrageous, I might lose *you* here. *Yeah, sure, a genie*, you're probably saying to yourself. But read on, because what I learned can change *your* life. Again I ask you, just suspend your disbelief for the moment. Later on you'll thank me. You might even write me into your will.

This genie wasn't like a skimpily clad Barbara Eden in *I Dream of Jeannie*. The genie that came out of the spray can was big. I'd say about six-foot-three, weighing maybe 250 pounds. And *Japanese*. In size, he reminded me of a Japanese Dick Butkus. In looks, his cousin could have been Oddjob, the henchman in the James Bond movie *Goldfinger*. Still, he looked stylish, wearing what appeared to be a gray pinstripe Italian suit. Those Japanese always know good fashion.

You might think that I was hallucinating. Heck, if I had had time to think, *I* would have thought that I was hallucinating. But this happened so quickly, I just stood there staring at this big genie.

"*Arigato go zai mas*," he said. I stared at him.

He probably could tell that I didn't understand a word. "Thank you very much," he said, translating for me.

I was starting to regain some composure. You know how sometimes you think of a zillion things in about a nanosecond? That's the way my mind was racing now. My brain examined and discarded everything from the possibility of hallucination to insanity to a combination of both. I discarded the thought that the pepperoni pizza I had the previous night could have caused this insanity—it had never caused those side effects before.

Before I could explore more in a second nanosecond, the big genie spoke again.

"I'm Darrell," he said, extending a hand for me to shake.

I reached out and shook it. It was *real flesh*. This guy wasn't one of those apparitions that you could see through. He was the real McCoy, even though he did somehow burst out of an aerosol can.

"Darrell?" I asked. Clearly that wasn't a Japanese name.

As if reading my thoughts, he said, "My real name is Yoshifumi, but I wanted to Americanize it for you."

Darrell? Maybe he wanted to prove to me that he could handle the r's and the l's. He did, flawlessly.

I introduced myself.

"Good to meet ya," he said. "You're probably wondering why I called this meeting." And then he laughed. "I've always wanted to say that line."

"What are you?" I asked, sort of blurting it out.

"Just what you thought I was when I came flying out of that aerosol can. A genie." Then he pulled open his suit coat and showed the Armani label. "Just a little bit more modern." Strangely, he spoke with a strong Brooklyn accent.

"So, pal," he said, "let's get on with it. You've got two wishes."

"I thought the deal was three wishes," I said.

"Ahh, you Americans. You always exaggerate, exaggerate, exaggerate. *Bigger! More!* Well, lemme tell you, pal, it has *always* been two wishes, always *will* be two wishes. So, what's it gonna be?"

I laughed. This whole thing was too crazy. Maybe pepperoni pizza does make you hallucinate. Maybe that's why kids love it so. They even order it with *extra* pepperoni. OK, I thought, since I'm here and since this guy appears to be a genie, I'll just play along with my hallucination until reality fades in.

"My first wish," I said, rolling my eyes

skyward, giving the appearance of thinking, "is that I want to have *three* wishes."

"A wise guy, eh?" he said. "This ain't no joking matter. In fact, your first wish is *not* going to be granted. And you forfeit that wish for being a wise guy." Obviously he didn't have much of a sense of humor.

"You're kidding, of course," I said.

"Nope. That's it. *One wish.* Take it or leave it."

He picked up the aerosol can and tossed it in his hand. "C'mon, let's take a walk. I'd like to stretch my legs." Off he went. I caught up to him and hustled to stay in lockstep, stride for stride.

"There are some things that you can't wish for," he said casually.

"I didn't realize that there were ground rules," I said.

"Oh yeah, whatd'ya think this is, winning the lottery or something?" Darrell said.

"Well, now that you mention it, yes."

"Nope. Not at all. Here are the ground rules, pal."

Darrell stopped and turned toward the ocean. "Beautiful, isn't it? Wow! I've been in that can a long time."

"The ground rules?" I reminded him.

"Oh yeah. Well, the first ground rule is that you can't ask for money."

"You can't?" I said.

"Don't look so disappointed, pal," Darrell said. "That's why this isn't like winning the lottery. If you want money, take some company public. Or, merge a company and then fire a lot of people. The Wall Street folks will love you and you can cash out your stock a little while later and make a fortune. But don't worry about the money as far as your wish is concerned. If you wish the right thing, the money will naturally take care of itself."

That was easy for him to say. I don't think he really needed any money. After all, he was a genie. He could just wish for things and they would come true. Like that Armani suit he was wearing. I can't imagine him sauntering into Barney's in New York City and plunking down two thousand dollars in cash for a suit when he could just blink it on.

For me, money hasn't been that easy. Sure, I make a decent living. But, you aren't going to see me buying any Major League team. Heck, I really can't afford season tickets to

Blazer games even though I have them. Each year it seems like I have to sell off more tickets to friends. I've even gone to the extreme of advertising in the classified section of the newspaper to sell tickets. There are forty-one home games; I sell off about thirty-five or thirty-six. So, it looks like *my* season ticket is five or six lousy games.

While I was thinking how unfair this ground rule was, the genie said, "There's a second ground rule."

I looked up at him.

"No women."

"No women? What do you mean?"

"Well, some guys would ask for some movie star to fall in love with them," Darrell said. "You know, a beautiful, rich and famous movie star becoming your love slave. Women aren't a part of the deal. That you have to work out for yourself. I'm a *business* genie. I'm a *specialist*."

Terrific, that's just terrific. I run across a genie and he can't provide me money or women.

The women part actually wasn't so bad. I'm married. Although someplace along the way we seemed to have hit a few speed bumps. That's why I played hooky from work and drove out to this lonely Oregon beach. I was thinking and walking and wondering why my life and my marriage were on a slow treadmill. I have to admit that while Darrell was explaining the second ground rule, another flash of thoughts appeared in a nanosecond—thoughts forged in the fantasy of wishing for some rich and famous movie star to fall in love with me. For just that nanosecond, it seemed pretty appealing and exciting.

"Anyplace around here where we can get something to eat?" Darrell asked.

I told him that there was a place to eat about a half mile up the beach.

"Let's go, I'm starved," Darrell said, picking up the pace. He walked as quiet as snow.

"Oh, by the way, you've got a week to come up with your wish," he said.

Chapter 2

Lewis and Clark set out in 1804 to find a water connection between the Missouri River and the Pacific Ocean. You know, sort of like a Mississippi River, but flowing from east to west.

They rode over plains that had no interstate highways.

Somehow they managed to find their way around and over mountains that would intimidate most of today's skiers.

They forded gushing rivers that had salmon the size of dogs leaping upstream.

They fought off Indians that didn't know they were trying to protect their land for future casinos.

And finally, after twenty-eight months of this stuff, they ended up looking the Pacific

Ocean right in the eye. And, while it was never written up in the history books, that's when they first saw Bill's Tavern.

"What's that?" Lewis asked Clark, pointing south down the beach.

"It must be a mirage," Clark said squinting. "Yeah, it's got to be a mirage. It looks like a *tavern*."

They were looking at a plank building. A sign was painted on the side: Bill's Tavern *Fresh Draft Beer*.

Sure, I'm exaggerating. But, it *seems* that Bill's Tavern has been there forever. If Lewis and Clark had wandered down the beach and walked into this mirage, the bar would have been filled with unemployed lumberjacks. That's where I took Darrell.

There were a few unemployed lumberjacks sitting at the bar. The four wood booths were empty. We walked across the old wood floor to a booth in the corner. If you looked carefully enough at the floor, you'd probably spot some ancient bloodstains from a time long ago when men were men and a fight was just good Friday night entertainment. That was, of course, before cable and ESPN.

The menu at Bill's was limited. Clam chowder. Cheeseburgers with potato chips. A ham sandwich. And chili. Take it or leave. And, oh yes, Guinness on tap.

The cheeseburgers were the best in the world. Don't even think about the fat content being about seventy percent. Think about the taste! And while you're at it, throw a couple of strips of bacon on it.

The locals glanced at Darrell. It's not too often they'll see a six-foot-three-inch, 250-pound Japanese guy dressed up like a fancy Italian. They were so focused on Darrell, I don't think they even saw me.

A scrawny guy with a ponytail walked over to our table. He was a former unemployed lumberjack and was now the bartender, waiter and cook. "What'll it be, fellas?" he asked.

Darrell didn't have to think. "A bowl of clam chowder, a bowl of chili, four cheese-burgers, two pints of Guinness," he said.

The bartender-waiter-cook nodded and turned to walk away.

"Wait a minute," Darrell said. "How about my friend?"

"I thought your order was for both."

Darrell said, "Nope."

The waiter looked at me. I said, "Cheese-burger and a pint of Bud for me."

After the beer was delivered, Darrell raised his glass to clink with mine. I raised mine. "To one wish," Darrell said. I nodded.

"So, pal, what do you do for a living?" Darrell asked.

"Why do you talk that way?" I asked, changing the subject.

"What way?"

"You know, you talk like you're from Brooklyn. *Pal* this, *pal* that. I know you didn't come from Brooklyn."

Darrell laughed. "I just like the sound of it. I speak 118 languages, but the one I like the best is Brooklynese."

"That's not a language, Darrell, that's an accent."

"So, sue me, pal. Now, what do you do for a living?"

"Real estate," I said.

"Invest? Commercial? Houses? What?"

"I'm a real estate salesman—houses," I said.

"How do you like it?" Darrell asked.

I shrugged. "It's a living."

The foam on Darrell's Guinness was settling down and he took a long swallow.

"Probably not too successful," he said, some of the foam on his lip.

"It's a living," I said.

"Well, there are three ways to the top in any business," he said. "This is true throughout the world. Always has been, always will be."

I took a long swallow from my Bud. Here was my genie with a Brooklyn accent pontificating about life! What does he know about life? He's been in a spray paint can.

"Is your father still alive?" he asked.

I nodded.

"Is he rich? Does he own his own business? Is it a *big* business?"

"No to each of those questions," I said. I drank some more Bud. The way I was cranking through this one, maybe I should have ordered two at a time like Darrell.

"That's too bad. That's the first way to the top. Inherit it. That's the best way, inherit it," Darrell said. "I know, some will say that if you inherit a fortune, it will deprive you of the *opportunity* of earning and doing. That may be true, but if *you* had inherited a fortune, you wouldn't be walking the beach alone. You'd have a huge home on the beach and you'd be walking with your mistress. Not bad, eh? But, it doesn't sound like this is your path to the top. How about your wife? She rich?"

"Nope."

"That's too bad. That's the second way to the top. Marry into it."

Darrell drained his first Guinness and started on his second. He sighed. He started to pat the pockets of his jacket, searching for something. Finally, he reached inside his jacket and fished out a cigar. He looked over at the bar. With all the unemployed lumberjacks smoking, it looked like a smoldering fire of leaves over there. Darrell took that as his right to light up. He puffed and puffed, exhaled, puffed some more. He just sat there smoking.

"OK, Darrell, you've got me going oh-for-two. I didn't inherit it and I didn't marry into it," I said, breaking his concentration on the cigar. "What's the third way to the top?"

"Do you have a mentor? You know, somebody you respect that gives you guidance?"

I shook my head no.

"Well, that's not so bad. Mentors are overrated as far as I am concerned. Sure, they can give you advice and make a few introductions for you, maybe give you a few shortcuts, but then you still gotta do it yourself anyway."

The ponytailed bartender brought over the bowl of clam chowder and the bowl of chili and placed them in front of Darrell. Darrell puffed on his cigar in between slurps from his chowder and chili.

"Your boss a good guy?" he asked.

"He's a jerk," I said, watching the smoke slide out of Darrell's mouth as he shoveled in chowder. "A real jerk."

"Well, that's OK too," Darrell said. "It would be better if you learned a lot from your boss, if he was an inspiration to you, if you respected him, if you liked him. But that's OK."

"What's OK about it?" I asked.

"The third way to the top. *Ride the right horse*. The right horse *could* be a powerful mentor. The right horse *could* be an inspiring boss. But, when it's all said and done, the right horse has to be *you*. *Ride the right horse*. Ride *yourself.*"

Yeah sure, I thought, ride the right horse. Ride me! The way I'm going, I'll ride myself right into oblivion.

Chapter 3

Have you ever seen a guy eat four greasy—deliciously so—cheeseburgers at one sitting? I hadn't either. Until Darrell. Interestingly, he didn't eat them one at a time. I don't mean that he tried to eat all four at the same time. Instead, he took a bite out of one. "*Umm-mmmmm,*" he said. Then he took a bite out of another. "*Ummmmmmm, good.*" Then a bite out of the third. Then the fourth. It's like he was alternating between steak and lobster and vegetables. Except he was alternating between cheeseburger, cheeseburger, cheeseburger and cheeseburger. Strange guy. Or, I guess you'd say strange *genie*.

The process continued, but he took second

bites out of the cheeseburgers in a different order than the first bites. A second bite out of the third cheeseburger, a second bite out of the first cheeseburger. These random single bites continued on until he had finished all the burgers. And the last bite was out of the first burger. Was he saving the best for last? Who knows? Darrell wasn't talking except for the occasional *Ummmmmmmm.*

The unemployed lumberjacks at the bar seemed impressed with Darrell. Not with his quirky style of eating—I don't think these guys were into style points for eating—but with the volume. They probably figured that he was one of those sumo wrestling guys.

While the last bite was in his mouth, Darrell said, "I'll be with you for the week."

"What do you mean?"

"Well, you've got a big decision to make," Darrell said, wiping his mouth with a paper napkin. "You might need some advice from somebody that has got experience in this type of stuff. That's me, pal. Nobody's more of an expert on wishes than me. So, wherever you go, I go."

He could tell that I was mulling this over.

"Don't worry," he said, "I won't get in the

way. Nobody will notice me, unless you want me to be noticed. Here, let me give you a little demonstration."

The ponytailed waiter arrived at the table to clear the dishes. "Anything else?" he asked.

I said, "Cup of coffee."

"What about your friend?" the waiter asked. I looked at Darrell. He just sat there smiling like a huge Japanese Cheshire cat.

"Ask him," I said. "He speaks English."

"Where did he go?" the waiter asked.

"He's right there," I said, pointing at Darrell.

The waiter looked at me as if I was having hallucinations from some freako recipe of drugs and cheeseburgers. Darrell kept smiling at me.

"I'll get you your coffee," the waiter said to me and walked back to the bar.

"See?" Darrell said.

"See what?" I said.

"That's the point. The waiter didn't see me. He thinks you're some wacko, by the way."

"You can make yourself *invisible*?" I asked.

Darrell nodded, smiling. "Among other

amazing things. I can turn it on and off like a faucet. I'd be a great act out in Las Vegas."

"Or bank robbing."

"It's a little trick I learned from Einstein, the disappearing," Darrell said.

"From *Albert* Einstein?"

"Who else? You think it would be *Ralph* Einstein?" Darrell asked. "Yep, old Albert was famous for developing the theory of relativity. But, that wasn't his greatest discovery. What was bigger than that was his discovery of *parallel worlds,* 'cept he died before he could prove the physics of it all."

"Parallel worlds?"

"Yeah, you know, like *time travel,*" Darrell said. "You don't need a machine or nothing like in H. G. Wells' book *The Time Machine*. That's what Einstein discovered. You see, he felt that human beings measure time the wrong way."

"How's that?"

"Humans measure time in seconds, minutes, hours, days and so forth," Darrell said. "Einstein measured time a different way and that's how he discovered time travel. He showed me how. That's where I was when that waiter came. I didn't really disappear into thin air. I just moved into the future by about five minutes. It's really pretty easy to do. Einstein found that out. With his little trick, you could travel to the future or the past just as easy as sitting here drinking a beer."

Darrell looked at his watch. Rolex, of course. He pointed to the hands on the watch and said, "This is the time you can understand. See the little hand? See the big hand? It's time we headed back to Portland, wouldn't you say?"

The drive was only an hour and a half, so a lot of people make day trips. I was one of those day-trippers. I had gone into the office at my usual time, about nine-thirty in the morning, and realized I just couldn't face the day of boredom and a jerk of a boss. Being in real estate, you have some real flexibility. You know, you can always be out canvassing for house listings. Or checking out some real estate, which could just as easily be the type of land found on a golf course or on a sandy public beach. It's all in the interpretation. So there I was, walking the lonely beach on a Wednesday, talking with a genie.

We left Bill's Tavern. Who knows what myths the unemployed lumberjacks would create about this giant Japanese guy who downed cheeseburgers as if they were potato chips.

We had to walk down the beach, back to where I parked my car in a public park.

"I'll drive," Darrell said, extending his hand for the keys to my Ford Taurus. At the time, this didn't seem unreasonable. After all, why not let the genie drive? With Darrell driving, I've never had a stranger or weirder drive. It would have stunned Rod Serling.

Chapter 4

If you were from New York City or Davenport, Iowa, and you took this road back to Portland during the daytime, you'd say this was the most scenic trip you had ever made.

You'd drive past mountains where trees grow up the sides so thickly that you can't see any rocks. You'd fly past tumbling streams that you knew had to be special fishing holes for somebody. Along the way, there were a couple of places that you could get coffee and food. Sometimes, I'd stop at one of these places to delay my return to Portland and all it didn't mean to me. I'd read the morning paper that I had stashed in my briefcase and drink enough coffee to put a buzz on a dead man.

At night, the scenic drive was pretty much defused. It was more like driving down a tunnel of darkness. The mountains and the great fishing holes were hidden in the blackness. The only thing you saw was the centerline of the road and occasionally some oncoming headlights. With Darrell at the wheel, my mind shifted into neutral. You know, that state where you're not thinking of anything and not noticing anything, but you're still alive. I was jolted out of this mind mushiness when Darrell pulled off the road.

"I gotta have some dessert and coffee," Darrell said. He parked the Ford in front of a diner.

At one time or another, I'd had coffee at each of the handful of restaurants scattered along the way back to Portland. This diner I had never seen before. Darrell must have made a wrong turn someplace.

"Where are we?" I asked.

"On the way back to Portland," Darrell said. He walked into the diner with me following.

The place was packed with people. Let me tell you, when you stop at one of these restaurants at night on your way back to Portland, you're lucky to see two or three people—and that includes the waitress. In this diner, every table and booth was taken. There were only two empty stools at the counter. We took those two places.

A beefy counterman came over to us. He was wearing a starched white T-shirt and khakis, and a white paper hat. The hat and T-shirt had a printed signature on them that looked like *Mack's*. Hair was coming out of every place that wasn't covered by the shirt and hat.

"Darrell! Long time no see!" the beefy guy said, extending his hand.

Darrell shook it. He introduced me and I shook the guy's hand too.

"Been traveling, Mack," Darrell said. *Traveling*, I thought, that's what you call going seven thousand miles in a spray paint can?

"Well, I've got just the dessert for you," Mack said. "It's something I've been working on. Also, I'm coming closer to perfecting my coffee."

"Mack's always trying to improve the best," Darrell told me. "He's got the best pie, but he's gonna make it better. He's got the best coffee, but he's gonna make that better too."

"So, business still looks great," Darrell said looking around the diner.

"All the time, it's busy. It *is* great!" Mack said with a big smile.

"Long hours?" Darrell asked.

"You bet. But it's funny, each day I have more energy than the previous day. It's like my work *feeds me energy*, ever since you taught me about *ewe*," Mack said. "Pie and coffee for you both?" Darrell nodded and Mack hustled off to the kitchen.

"He's . . . he's . . . one of yours?" I asked.

Darrell nodded yes.

"What's this about you teaching him about *you*? That doesn't make much sense to me."

"Ewe," Darrell corrected me. Then he spelled it out, "E-W-E."

"Ewe?" I asked.

"Ewe."

"Like a female sheep?"

"Nope. And it's not the language of the people that inhabit Ghana."

"What's that?"

"Ewe. That's what their language is called," Darrell said. Then he spelled it again,

"E-W-E. Ewe. I know their language too. Wanna hear?"

I shook my head no. "Let's get back to what Mack said, 'You taught me about ewe.' What's E-W-E?"

Mack set down cups of steaming coffee in front of Darrell and me. The aroma reached up and grabbed my nostrils. "Wow," I said, "that's good enough just to smell." Mack smiled. I took a sip. It tasted even better than it smelled. "How could coffee be *this* good?" I asked.

"*Esia ye nye coffe nyuitor le xexame*," Darrell said.

"Pardon?" I said.

"That was Ewe for 'it's the best coffee in the world.'"

"So, Darrell, tell me about this E-W-E."

Darrell sipped his coffee. "Let's talk about work ethic."

"Work ethic? What's that got to do with E-W-E?"

"The W in E-W-E stands for Work. The second E stands for Ethic. Work Ethic," Darrell said.

Mack brought over two pieces of lemon meringue pie. "You know how Key West is famous for its key lime pie?" Mack asked. "Well, that stuff tastes like vanilla compared to my lemon meringue pie. Taste it. I get special lemons from Israel. They're flown in right after they're picked."

Darrell and I both pushed a fork into our piece of pie. Wow! If you ever wanted lemon in a pie, this was it. It sucked in your cheeks until they touched each other inside your mouth. I tempered the taste with some of that terrific coffee.

"I used to think *work ethic* was everything," Darrell said. "You know, the harder you work, the better you'll do. I even thought that work ethic was a kind of *random determinism*."

"Random determinism?" I asked.

"Sure, an accident," Darrell said, "just like there are some people that are born to throw a baseball one hundred miles an hour. You, me, Mack, all these people in this restaurant can't throw a baseball like that. You have to be born with the right muscle structure, bones, everything. You have to be born to it; it's not something that you can develop. And, the best that I can tell, it's *random*."

I ate another piece of pie. Wow again!

"If it was handed down from generation to generation," Darrell continued, "how come the *sons* of all the great pitchers throughout baseball history can't throw the great fastball? Where's Nolan Ryan's son? I don't know, but he's not pitching in the Major Leagues."

I thought about that. I thought about great pro basketball players. Michael Jordan. Larry Bird. Magic Johnson. Their fathers weren't former pro players. Heck, Jordan, Bird and Magic came from small towns, not from the large cities where the greatest basketball was supposed to be played. *Random determinism.*

"I thought the same thing with work ethic," Darrell said, taking a huge piece of pie on his fork. "It was like being born with a great pitching arm. If you didn't have a great arm, you couldn't develop one. Sure, you might have been pretty good in Little League or even the low Minors, but to make it big-time you had to be born with a great arm. Same with work ethic. If you didn't have a great work ethic, you couldn't develop one. Sure, you could develop a *decent* work ethic, but you had to be *born* with a great work ethic. *Random determinism.*"

"So who wants a great work ethic?" I

asked. "I'd rather have a great arm. That would be even better than having a genie grant you one wish. Then I could have money and movie stars."

Darrell looked at me out of the corner of his eye. "You making fun again? I can take that one wish away, you know, pal. Then you got nothing."

"Hey, Darrell, sense of humor, *sense of humor*. Americans have that, you know. Relax, pal."

He looked at me trying to determine if I was putting him on, if he was being made fun of. "That's funny?" he asked.

"That's funny," I said. I didn't know what he was referring to as funny. But now Darrell thought whatever it was was funny. He let out a big cackle.

"Now, I've seen some great work ethic around the world," Darrell said. "My own countrymen have a great work ethic. Twelve-hour days, devotion to the company. It's a *country* of great work ethic. A lot of it is forced, but they put on a pretty good show of work. Sort of like the guy that doesn't have a great arm, but he battles his way through the Minor Leagues to finally reach his pinnacle, triple A."

"Mack was like that," Darrell said, pointing his fork at the big beefy guy now waiting on somebody at the end of the counter. "Worked hard. Lotta, lotta hours. What'd it get him?"

"Looks like a pretty good business," I said.

"Nah," Darrell said, "I'm not talking about now. I'm talking about then. Mack worked hard, really hard. All it got him was a little bit older and deeper in debt. Nah, a great work ethic is overrated. I've seen people that by random determinism had great—really great—work ethics, but it wasn't enough. Sure, they might have been a little more successful than if they hadn't had that fabulous work ethic, but not enough more successful for it to count."

Before I could ask Darrell to explain what the first E in E-W-E was, he got up and straightened out his suit. "Let me show you something," he said.

I hadn't quite finished my lemon meringue pie. "C'mon," he said, walking between the tables toward the wall across the room. The wall was a floor-to-ceiling mirror, making the room seem even bigger.

Where was he going? I thought. There wasn't an exit at that end of the diner, nor were the restrooms located at that end. He must be going to see somebody. I turned back to my lemon meringue pie, scooped up the last piece and turned just in time to see Darrell walk through the mirror. That's right, *he walked through the mirror and disappeared.*

I looked around the room. Nobody had seemed to notice. They were busy eating, drinking coffee, talking and laughing.

I walked to the mirror. About a foot away from it, I stopped and just stared at the glass, seeing if I could see through it. I couldn't. I just saw myself staring into the mirror. I reached out and touched the mirror. My hand didn't go through. All I felt was the mirror.

Darrell's arm reached out of the mirror, grabbed me by the wrist and yanked me through. I'll assume you've never walked through a mirror, so you might be wondering about the experience. It was underwhelming. It was just like being yanked from one room to the next.

The room I was yanked to was exactly the same as the room that I had been yanked from. Except it was different. Instead of a diner filled with hungry, laughing people, there were only two old guys sitting at the counter.

Darrell pulled me over to a booth.

"Remember what I told you about Einstein?" Darrell asked me.

I nodded, "Parallel worlds."

"Right. Maybe there is hope for you, pal."

Mack came over from behind the counter. He looked the same, but there was something different. It's not that he had shaved his beefy hairy arms or anything. He just didn't *seem* the same. He seemed tired, worn down.

"What can I get you?" he asked. I looked at Darrell. Mack hadn't recognized Darrell. Darrell's the type of guy that if you met him, you'd remember him. *Parallel worlds.* I was starting to get it.

Darrell said, "Coffee and a piece of pie."

I said, "Just coffee for me."

Mack walked back to the counter.

"He didn't recognize you," I said to Darrell. "What parallel world are we in, anyway?"

"Two years ago," Darrell said. "See any difference in Mack?"

"Yeah. Over there," I said, pointing to the other world beyond the mirror, "he seemed to have so much *passion*, so much *joy* running the diner. Over here, he seems like he's got the flu.

You know, like he would like to just leave and go to bed."

"That's not all that's different," Darrell said. "Wait'll you taste the coffee and see the pie."

As if on cue, Mack brought the coffee and a wedge of a brownish thing on a plate. He laid down the check and went back to the counter.

"You're probably wondering what that is," Darrell said, pointing to the thing on the plate. "Apple. Apple pie."

"You're going to eat it?" I asked. It looked like Mack had put a dog turd with whipped cream on a plate and put it on the table as some weird practical joke.

"Nope," Darrell said. "God knows I could down a whole pie, maybe two or three, but I'll pass on this one." Darrell pushed the piece of pie to the far corner of the booth, beyond our field of vision.

"Mack puts in more hours now than he does on the other side of that mirror," Darrell said. "Not that he takes much time off over there, but here he practically lives at this joint. The great work ethic is wasted. That's not E-W-E."

That led me to ask what the first E in E-W-E was.

"*Effective*," Darrell said, "as in *Effective* Work Ethic. E-W-E isn't just a mountain of hours. If you're just putting in the long hours and not being terrifically effective for all that time spent, then you're just like an observer watching your career go no place. And then one day your career ends and you, the observer, say, 'That's it?' That's all, folks. Then you'd just observe yourself doing nuthin' in retirement— going out to the mailbox to fetch your mail would be your big event of the day—then you die. I can show you better than tell you. Mack is 'Exhibit A' regarding E-W-E. You're probably wondering what happened to Mack, how come he changed?"

I nodded.

"A whipped cream can," he said.

"Huh?"

"One day, somebody ordered a piece of apple pie—he must've been a stranger—and Mack shook up a new can of whipped cream. He shook it and shook it, pressed the nozzle and *voila!* Yours truly popped out into his awful kitchen."

"Whipped cream can?"

"The vessel ain't important," Darrell said. "After all, you can't find too many Aladdin lamps like the old days. You gotta take what you can get to circulate."

I wanted to ask him how he jumped from vessel to vessel, but he jumped up from the booth and said, "Let's go, you've seen enough here. I got something else to show you."

He threw a five-dollar bill on the table and walked like a man on a mission to where else but the mirror. I quickly got up from the booth, took one brief glance at the apple pie in the corner of the table, winced a little bit and easily, casually, as if I had been doing it for my entire life, walked right through the mirror.

When I was halfway in the diner that I was leaving and halfway in the place I was stepping into, I heard, *"Hey, Darrell! Good to see you, friend."*

It was Mack. By now, Mack was probably used to Darrell walking through mirrors.

The diner was about half full. I followed Darrell to two open stools at the counter.

By the time I got to the stool, Mack had already delivered two cups of coffee.

"Who's your friend?" Mack asked.

Darrell introduced me again and we shook hands again.

"Try the coffee," Mack said. I would like to have said that he was beaming, but that sounds a little too corny. But, he *was* beaming, almost as if he was showing off a grandchild.

"That's very good, Mack," Darrell said after he took a sip. "Very, very good. How did you do it? Your other stuff was really quite lousy, you know."

"Well, it wasn't easy, but it was easy, d'you know what I mean?"

I didn't know what he meant.

"What did you do first?" Darrell asked.

"Well, after you . . . ah . . . left . . . after we first met, I stayed late in the kitchen after it closed. I just sat there," he said. "I just sat there looking. I didn't like what I saw. You know, over the years this kitchen got pretty greasy and grimy. The next day I rented one of those steam cleaners and that night I worked all night long cleaning the place. Heck, it looked brand new. Just getting rid of all that grease and grime made my coffee a little bit better."

I glanced over at the service window that opened to the kitchen. From what I saw inside the kitchen, it *still* looked brand new.

I took another sip of coffee. It wasn't quite as good as the coffee that Darrell and I had in the 'first' diner. And, the aroma didn't navigate as well up into your nostrils. But, it was a darned good cup of coffee.

"The second thing I did was figure out how I could get coffee direct from Java, Indonesia," Mack said.

"Why Indonesia?" I asked.

"That's the best coffee in the world," Mack said. "But you just can't get it from your normal suppliers. I found a supplier that had some, then I bought some Kona coffee, and then I bought some special Brazilian stuff."

He then turned to Darrell and said, "I've been working with different blends since you left. I'm getting close, I think, to the best cup of coffee in the world."

Darrell nodded. "Close."

"But, it'll get better," Mack said. "I worked out a way to get *fresh* coffee beans—I mean *really* fresh. Through the Internet, I found a coffee grower in Java, Indonesia, that will

FedEx coffee beans to me the *very* day that they are ready. I get my first shipment tomorrow. I can hardly wait to try it; I feel like a kid waiting for Christmas."

"That must be expensive," I said.

"Sure it is," Mack said. "But, you know, these 'coffee bars' are charging three bucks for a cup of coffee. I can charge a lot less than that, make a decent profit and you'll be getting the best cup of coffee in the world."

Mack saw a customer signal for more coffee. "Excuse me for a minute," Mack said, grabbing the coffeepot and scooting over to the customer.

"What time is it?" I asked Darrell.

Darrell looked at his Rolex. "Nine thirty-seven," he said.

"No, I don't mean what clock time, I mean *when is this* . . . you know, in Einstein's parallel worlds, which world are we in?"

"*Ah-so*," Darrell said. "About two months after that," he said, motioning back toward the mirror that we had just walked through. "And about two years before . . . before the 'first' diner."

I nodded. If anyone had overheard us,

there was no way they would understand what we were talking about. I wasn't sure of this whole thing myself, but I was trying to roll with the punches the best I could.

Mack was back. "I'm working on a lemon meringue pie," Mack said. "It's not ready yet for you to try, but I'm getting closer. I want to make my lemon meringue pie more famous than key lime pie. It's all in the lemons, you know. I'm experimenting with a different lemon from Israel. Flown direct to me."

Mack saw another customer and he was off like a greyhound.

"See the difference?" Darrell asked me. "The one constant thing in the three Mack's Diners that we visited via parallel worlds was *work ethic*. Mack worked hard in all three. He's no slouch. But in the 'present' diner, and this one, he's been using E-W-E. *Effective* Work Ethic. Can you see the difference?"

"Sure. It's like walking into a dark room and turning on a light. Why? It can't be just coffee and lemon meringue pie."

Darrell laughed. "You'll see."

"Let's go," Darrell said. "See ya, Mack," he yelled, dropping a few dollars on the counter.

He pivoted and walked toward the door with me following.

"Hey, don't we have to go through the mirror again?" I asked.

"New trick," he said. "Pay attention." We stepped through the open doorway into the night. There was my car. We got in and drove off into the dark night, leaving this mysterious diner. As before, Darrell drove.

"I don't know what his wish was," I said, "or his *two* wishes—you probably didn't penalize him one wish—but he sure is a lively guy. It's strange, I don't equate *joy* with people working in a diner, but he sure has it."

"That he does, that he does," Darrell said.

After a few minutes of silence and mulling over what I had just seen, I said, "I bet I know what his two wishes were."

"You think so, eh? Whatd'ya want to lose?" Darrell asked. "Would you want to go *double or nothing* on your one wish?"

I had already lost half of my wishes, so I thought I better not risk the last one. A wish in the hand is better than two in the bush, I guess, so I declined.

Darrell laughed. "You would have lost."

"Coffee and lemon meringue pie," I said. "Mack wanted to have the best coffee and lemon meringue pie in the world."

"Wrong on both counts," Darrell said. "Mack *will* have the best coffee and *will* have the best lemon meringue pie, but those weren't his wishes. Not even close."

When we arrived on the outskirts of Portland, Darrell pulled to the side of the road. "See that Denny's across the street?" he said, pointing. I nodded. "Pick me up there at ten tomorrow morning."

He jumped out of the car. The last words I heard from him that night were *Grand Slam breakfasts*. That's plural. Each Grand Slam breakfast has, I think, three eggs, three pancakes, three pieces of bacon and three sausages. If Darrell mirrored his breakfast eating to his cheeseburger extravaganza, he would knock down twelve eggs, twelve pancakes, twelve pieces of bacon and twelve sausages tomorrow morning. And maybe a partridge in a pear tree.

He was out of sight by the time I slid over behind the steering wheel. Where he was going to sleep that night, God only knows. It wasn't going to be in that aerosol paint can. The can was still lying on the floor in the back of my car. That would probably be a safer place for me to sleep. My wife sure wasn't going to believe this.

Chapter 5

The next morning, there he was, standing in front of Denny's. He didn't look any bigger. He wore a different Italian suit. It must be great to be a genie and carry your wardrobe in a wish.

Before I could pull a U-turn, he sprinted into an opening in the traffic as if he were trying to go from first base to third on a single to right. He would have made it standing up. Within a flash he was climbing into the passenger seat of my car. Wow, he could move fast for a big guy—a big guy who had probably put on an eating exhibition that the waitresses would be talking about for weeks to come.

"Let's go," Darrell said.

"Where to?" I asked.

He told me to go to a large office building downtown.

I didn't question the destination. After all, if you buy into the genie thing at all, then you find that you buy in all the way. Large office building it is.

After we parked in the basement of the large office building, we took the elevator to the tenth floor. It was a brokerage house.

In the lobby was one of those electronic ticker machines that stock symbols and prices scroll along. To me, it might as well have been written in Sanskrit. Darrell, however, stood there watching it, nodding, smiling.

"You can read that?" I asked Darrell.

"Yep," he said, "that's another language. I didn't even count that in the 118 languages I know. But this one makes the most money."

"You play the market?" I asked.

"Sure," Darrell said. "I make a lot of money every day, even when the market is down."

If there ever was a sure thing in this world, I thought, Darrell had it. Take a little trip into the future, look at *The Wall Street Journal*, come back and make a fortune. I didn't play the stock market, but with this type of a deal I'd learn real fast how to read those abbreviations flitting across the bottom of the screen.

"Can you give me a couple of tips?" I asked.

"I am," Darrell said. "That's why I'm here with you."

"No . . . I mean *stock* tips."

Darrell laughed and said, "If you were a stock, would you buy yourself right now?"

I snorted a laugh.

"I'm serious," Darrell said, "no jokes. Let me ask you again: *If you were a stock, would you buy yourself right now?*"

I thought about that for a moment. I'm sorry to say that I probably wouldn't. I'm not sure I'd classify myself as a loser stock, but I sure ain't a high flyer. Better to put my money in certificates of deposit than myself.

Darrell didn't wait for me to think any more. "How about Mack?" Darrell asked. "If he were a stock, would you buy him now?"

"Sure," I answered. "There's a lot of upside with Mack."

"Well, *I* would buy stock in you," Darrell said. "The market in you is depressed, been depressed for a long time. But, you've got that one wish. If you wish for the correct thing, your stock will skyrocket. You'll see."

Darrell turned to the receptionist, mentioned somebody's name and within a minute he said to me, "Let's go."

We walked toward a corner office. We navigated through a sea of cubicles. Each one was manned by a sharply dressed guy in suspenders with a phone attached to his ear. *They* had hot tips, at least that's what they were saying. I'd take their hot tip over Darrell's tip of buying me. The place was like a madhouse.

Across this sea of cubicles, Darrell waved to a woman. She was just finishing up a conversation with several men in suspenders. She was attractive, probably in her late thirties, wearing a conservative skirt and blouse and heels.

She started to come toward us. It's difficult to describe how she walked. It was like she was gliding—so smooth, but quick, confident, vibrant. She stopped a couple of times to quickly talk to a broker. You could just *feel* her presence from across the room. I assumed she was the secretary to whoever had that corner office. I tell you, that guy sure had a nice-looking secretary.

"Darrell! How are you doing?" the woman said, hugging him.

Darrell introduced me to her and we shook hands. I was dying for a cup of coffee, and I was about to ask her if she could get me one when she and Darrell walked into the corner office. She sat behind the big desk.

"Monica runs the place," Darrell said.

"Can I get you some coffee?" Monica asked, smiling.

I said, "Uh . . . yes . . . thank you . . . black."

Monica got up and walked over to a table that had a thermal pitcher. She poured two cups and delivered them to us.

As she sat down, the phone on her desk rang.

"Excuse me," Monica said, "I've been expecting this one call. We're closing on a big deal. Stay right there, it'll just be a minute."

I watched her as she was closing this big deal. She was talking calmly as if she were chatting with a friend. If this was a big deal, she sure didn't show it with negative emotions. In fact, she looked like she was having a terrific time. Even when she pecked some numbers on the computer, she did it with a quiet flair. I was having fun just watching her. That's how you make a big deal in this business, I guess. I heard her say, "OK, it's done. Thank you, Phil. This is a great investment for you."

If you're a salesperson, it's sort of a reflex to look at numbers on somebody's desk. I can even read things upside down. I don't consider this spying. It's more like being professionally nosy. It's a tough habit to break. In this case I didn't even have to read things upside down; I was able to see some of the numbers on the computer screen.

What jumped out to me was $14,000,000. She had just booked an order for fourteen million dollars worth of *something*. I don't know what stockbrokers earn on a deal, but to me, this certainly *was* a big deal. She handled the deal so confidently, it was like she was making a deal for $140 instead of fourteen *million* dollars.

A salesperson's eyes will also stray to look at things on walls. While she was on the phone, I scanned Monica's walls. There weren't any dead trophy fish hanging on the wall. There were, however, two diplomas. One was a college diploma. The second one showed that Monica had attended a Dale Carnegie course. Now why would she have that diploma up there next to her college diploma?

Her desktop was pristine except for two things. The keyboard for her computer, and a highly unusual teapot. It looked old, really old, and like it came from Europe or someplace far away. The pot sat on a highly varnished block of wood.

After she hung up, Monica pushed a button on her phone.

"Monica doesn't have anybody screen her phone calls," Darrell said, referring to the button that she had pushed on the phone.

"That's right," Monica said. "I started in this business as a secretary—or as they say nowadays, executive assistant—to the person that had this office. I knew that the time wasted on phone tag is enormous. I vowed that if I ever became a 'big-shot,' I'd eliminate that phone tag. I don't want anybody screening my calls."

Heck, even I, as a real estate salesman, have somebody to answer my phone. I *liked* somebody screening my calls. There were a lot of times I didn't want to talk to certain people. If somebody didn't screen my calls, I'd have to talk to those people when I didn't want to. It was a lot better for an executive assistant to say that I was out of the office and ask if she could take a message. If I ever became a big-shot, I'd surely have two or three assistants answering my phones.

"What about people that don't like voice mail?" I asked. I hated voice mail. It was like leaving a message in a black hole.

She pushed a couple of buttons on her phone. Her voice mail message played, "I'm not available right now, but if you leave your name and phone number, I'll get back to you within two hours. If you need immediate assistance, press the pound sign. Thank you for calling."

"Two hours?" I asked.

"*Within* two hours," she said, "and I never *not* return a call within two hours. Even when I'm traveling, I call in for my voice messages every two hours."

"Do you get many unwanted calls?" Darrell asked.

"I get some from people trying to sell something I don't want," Monica said, "but if they're good, really good on the phone, I have them come in. *They* might be a good candidate to be a broker here. That's how I'm getting promoted to the main office in New York—by finding great people and not doing anything to them that would screw them up."

"*Ah-so*," Darrell said. "Congratulations on your promotion. If I may ask, what position is it?"

"Executive vice president of our North America division," she said.

Wow, I thought, that was impressive. Executive vice president! And, she got me coffee! She didn't seem to be tough like some of the women executives that I had met. She just seemed like a nice woman . . . an *attractive* nice woman.

"I attribute a lot of my success to ewe." Monica said.

Darrell looked at me and spelled it out. "E-W-E, not Y-O-U."

Monica smiled at me and said, "Yes, I'm one of Darrell's disciples. I found Darrell when I was rummaging through a garage sale. I saw this old teapot. I liked it. I bought it for fifty cents. Unlike Aladdin who tried to clean his lamp, I just set mine down in the back of my car.

Then I got the scare of my life when Darrell popped up in the rearview mirror. I almost drove off the road.

"Then I learned about E-W-E. I first used E-W-E to learn how to become the best broker on the floor," Monica said. "Then, when I moved into management, I found that most of the skills that made me a great broker were not the same skills that could make me a great manager. I tried to use those skills when I first became a manager, but most of the people here thought I was a bitch. I *hate* that word. But they were right. I used E-W-E to develop the skills I would need to manage. That was a key to my promotion—to manage people so they would maximize their abilities. I got those people involved in E-W-E."

We chatted a little bit more, and then Darrell stood up and said, "Well, Monica, we don't want to take up any more of your time. I just wanted to stop by and say hello. You're doing terrific. I'm really proud of you. By the way, is there an office I can borrow to make a few phone calls?"

Monica gave him directions to the office for visiting executives.

After some good-byes and nice-to-meet-you's, we wove our way out through the madhouse.

"So, did Monica wish her way to the top?" I asked. "There aren't too many women in this industry. So it seems she must have had some extra help, like a wish or *two*."

"You're right, there aren't too many women in this industry and there are far fewer in the executive suite. She did have a wish and then she rode the right horse, *herself*. Even with the wish, it wasn't easy, believe me. Let me show you."

Darrell led the way to a closed office door. "Here we are," he said. "C'mon in."

I assumed it was the office for visiting executives. We stepped in.

The office was sparsely furnished with a desk, chair, phone and fax machine.

"OK," Darrell said, not even sitting down, "follow me."

We walked out the same door we had come in through.

It looked the same. Guys in the cubicles were still talking on the phone, they were still wearing suspenders. There was one difference.

Monica was in a cubicle. Well, I thought, here we go again in parallel worlds.

She looked different. Yes, she was younger, but that wasn't the big difference. She was dressed almost like a man. Slacks. Blazer. Even suspenders.

Monica spotted Darrell coming out of the office. She went over to him and shook his hand. Darrell introduced us again.

Monica offered to buy us both a cup of coffee. As we walked through the maze of cubicles to an empty lunchroom at the end of the office, Darrell whispered to me, "Seven years ago." I nodded. I was getting a real feel now for this parallel worlds stuff. Becoming a veteran, in fact.

After getting us coffee, Monica said to Darrell, "It's so difficult, Darrell, moving from secretary to broker."

I was impressed that Monica had the ability to make that move. That should have been enough by itself.

"What's so difficult about it?" Darrell asked.

"The men," Monica said. "This is like a fraternity. I've tried to fit in, but I'm a *woman*, and the only thing a woman is good for in a fraternity is to *party*."

"So, you've decided to *follow the followers*," Darrell said. "I see you've tried to lose your femininity. That type of thinking will only help you lose your focus."

"I'm just trying to fit in better," Monica said.

"Won't work," Darrell said. "Yes, by trying to be one of the guys, you might fit in a little better, but your wish won't come true. I'm not saying you should dress like a hooker, but be yourself and don't lose your femininity in the process. Go back to the lube jobs, oil changes and tune-ups of your wish, Monica. People respect success, people respect people that have a *passion* for their job, regardless of gender, race or religion. When you worry about gender, even though it is a real issue, you *lose some of the passion* for the job."

Lube jobs, oil changes, tune-ups? What in the world was Darrell talking about?

"You're right, Darrell, as always," Monica said. "I can see I've been getting off track a bit on 'being one of the boys.' I feel better already. I gotta run, make some more phone calls."

We left our half-filled cups of coffee and walked back to the bullpen. Darrell and I made the switch back to the present by walking into the office for visiting execs and then walking out. It was that easy.

Back in the car, Darrell said, "It is more difficult in this world for women in business. Difficult in your country, *really* difficult in my country. This is true with any minority, African-Americans, Asians, gays—you name the minority, it is tougher for them. It *is* more difficult for them. Laws have been passed to make it a level playing field, and we like to believe there is a level playing field, but there isn't. It is still more difficult for women and minorities.

"Women shouldn't be considered a minority, but in the executive ranks they are. Some women respond by giving up. Others respond by being artificially aggressive. They try to act tough, be tough. But, that act distorts their abilities, distorts who they really are. Yes, the degree of difficulty was ramped up a few notches for Monica, but you saw her success. Unfortunately they have to stay *more* focused— they shouldn't have to because they are women, but there is a big benefit of being more focused.

You've seen the results with Monica. She's one of thousands of women that are proving they can make it to the top, that it *is* possible, even though they have to have more discipline, more focus."

"What was that stuff about lube jobs, oil changes and tune-ups?" I asked. "You lost me there. Were you talking about her car?"

Darrell laughed. "Funny," Darrell said, "now *that's funny*." He laughed some more.

When he was down to the giggling stage, Darrell said, "Let's go out to the airport."

Chapter 6

The airport was a mess. There was massive construction going on. Cars inched through the detours. There would be some sprinters in dark-blue pinstripe suits catching the flights today.

We parked in the short-term lot and walked to the terminal. Yes, you could see it, quite a few of the people were late, walking as if the floor was a treadmill that had been stepped up a couple of notches.

Once inside the terminal, it seemed *everybody* was on a hopped-up treadmill. Even the crowd waiting in line to get ticketed. Sure, they didn't move, but their fidgeting was all up-tempo.

"C'mon over here," Darrell said, motioning to me. "I want you to see this."

I walked over to where Darrell was standing. It was between the ropes that separated the coach passengers from those in first class. It seemed like there were a thousand people in the coach line and two or three in the first class line.

"Watch this," Darrell said, nodding toward the ticket agents.

Several of the agents were clearly frazzled. I guess anybody in that position would be. One agent wasn't. It looked like *he* was having fun. He even greeted each passenger with a smile and a hello.

This agent was about fifty years old. This probably sounds weird, but he reminded me of an in-the-flesh Frosty the Snowman. This agent didn't have a button nose or two eyes made of coal, but he had the presence of Frosty. You know, cheery. Happy. Jolly. And boy, his hands were a blur on the computer keyboard. He could have made a fortune as a three-card monte dealer on the sidewalks of New York.

It seemed that once he took a passenger's ticket, his hands had a mind of their own as he was talking, even joking, with the passenger. I saw other agents doing a modern version of the hunt-and-peck typing system. And they were deep in concentration. Or they just didn't want to talk to the passengers. After all, who would want to talk to these hyped-up, sweating, nervous passengers? Punch out the ticket and get them out of here! But as fast as they would like to get them out of there and out of their sight, Frosty was really cranking them through faster. A lot faster. If he were being paid by the piece on some assembly job, he'd be making a fortune.

"Pretty interesting, eh?" Darrell said. I nodded. If I hadn't seen it myself, it would be difficult to believe that one agent could handle as many passengers as at least two other agents. It's not like the other agents were rookies or dullards; they looked experienced, and they sure looked like they were working hard. It's just that Frosty practically whisked the customers through like magic.

"Well, watch this," Darrell said. "This will really challenge George. This will slow him down." He nodded toward an ancient Japanese man as the old man inched, step by little quivering step, to the counter in front of Frosty. "I don't think this fella knows English too much."

George. Well, if a movie company was looking for somebody to play Frosty, George was it.

When the little Oriental man had finally reached the counter, Frosty . . . er . . . George bowed slightly.

I could hear George's greeting. It sounded like "Ohio go zai mas."

"Good morning," Darrell translated.

The Japanese man said something I couldn't hear clearly, but I knew it wasn't English.

Before the Japanese man could hand his ticket over the counter, George whipped out a business card from his shirt pocket. With two hands, George held the card out to the old man. As he extended his arms so that the old man could take the card, George bowed again, his eyes diverted downwards.

"One side of the card is printed in English," Darrell said, "the other side in Japanese. He's handing that old man the Japanese side up."

The old man took the card and bowed also. It was then business as usual for George. George took the man's ticket and within a microsecond his fingers raced over the keyboard. George then in one fluid motion slapped a destination sticker on the handle of the old man's suitcase that was placed in the slot between agents. In almost that same motion he whisked the suitcase onto the conveyor belt and turned back to pull out the man's boarding pass from the printer. It was as if George was a sleight-of-hand magician who made a suitcase disappear and a boarding pass appear. All the while, George was speaking to the man in Japanese. A three-card monte dealer would be stunned at the quickness.

George then squeezed through the slot where the old man's suitcase had been, gently took the man by the elbow and helped him navigate through the crowd. Once he was in the clear, George bowed deeply; the old man bowed back and went tottering off. George stood there watching him disappear into the crowd. Only then did he head back to the counter.

I looked back at the counter. The same passengers that had been working with the other agents were still there. Some sagged against the counter, waiting. Others impatiently tapped their feet as if that could speed up the process. While these passengers were waiting, fidgeting, sweating, George had processed his elderly non-English-speaking passenger, who could have been a real logjam. In fact, he had processed this old gentleman faster than the other agents had processed their customers. Amazing.

There was another amazing thing about this scene. If Darrell hadn't had me stand there and watch this whole thing like it was a baseball game, I'm sure I wouldn't have noticed George from the other agents. His movements weren't hurried, they weren't herky-jerky, he wasn't perspiring, he wasn't out of breath. In fact, it looked like he was just taking his time. And yet, he was processing passengers about twice as quickly as any other agent.

"He's one of yours?" I asked Darrell.

Darrell nodded. "You're getting smarter."

"When did . . . ah . . . you and he . . . meet?" I asked.

Darrell laughed. "About five years ago, but what you're really interested in is *how* did we meet. Right?"

"Well, sure," I said. "With me, you come out of a can of spray paint. With Mack, it was a can of whipped cream. With Monica, it was an old teapot."

"With George, I was in a can of STP," Darrell said.

"Can of STP?"

"Yep, a good old can of STP," Darrell said. "Slippery stuff, you know. Really, *really* slippery. George was going to add it to his crankcase to try to save his old Plymouth from getting a three-hundred-dollar valve job. He popped the top of the STP and *voila! Here's Johnny!*"

We watched for a couple of minutes more. Darrell looked at his Rolex and said, "George is going to be on break in about fifteen minutes. I'd like to introduce you to him."

"I'd like that," I said.

"In the meantime, follow me, I want to show you something," Darrell said, pivoting away from our vantage point like he was on skates. Man, this guy was nimble for a big guy.

As usual, I had to take a lot of quick steps to catch up to Darrell. Like a bowling ball barreling down a lane, he was heading straight for a gray metal door that had *Maintenance* stenciled on it. Darrell reached into his pocket and pulled out a large ring with about twenty keys on it.

He thumbed through them, finding the one that he wanted, and inserted it into the lock. He opened the door and politely ushered me inside.

It was a small room filled with stuff that you would think would be there like mops, buckets, an old-fashioned carpet sweeper. We could barely stand in the room without bumping into each other. Facing the door that we entered was another door. Darrell thumbed through the keys again and inserted one into the lock of the second door.

He opened it and again politely ushered me through. I stepped over a bucket and into the terminal. Uh-oh, here we go *time traveling* again. What I saw was the same Portland airport terminal, but it was different, a lot different. It was smaller, the carpeting was worn in places, there weren't nearly as many travelers and there was no construction going on at all.

"Six years ago," Darrell said, in answer to the question mark on my face. "Nice little airport," he added, and he was off again like a dog chasing after a bone with me scrambling behind him.

We ended up at the vantage point where we had been observing George just moments before. It looked about the same except there were fewer travelers and fewer ticket agents. But, you know something, *everybody* looked the same as in the previous terminal except for George. Now he looked just as harried as the other agents. They looked as harried as the travelers.

I watched George work. He didn't greet people. He just waited for them to hand him their ticket.

When George got the ticket in his hand, he looked at the computer as if it should be doing something on its own. George's fingers pecked at the keyboard. He put his hand up to his chin while he stared at the computer screen. He tapped out something else on the computer. He stared again. The passenger looked at his watch about every twenty seconds. My, how time doesn't fly. Eventually, the passenger was on his way, pushing himself into a spastic airport trot, and George waited for the next passenger's ticket.

"Well, whatd'ya think?" Darrell asked.

"His boss must have jumped all over him at some point," I said.

"Oh, really," Darrell said. "Why do you say that?"

"You can just tell. Here he's moving in slow motion. Over there," I said, pointing to the maintenance door, "he's really hustling. Over there he's working twice as hard as anybody else and I bet he gets the same pay."

"So it was his boss?"

"Yep, probably."

"You know, you're really missing something," Darrell said. "What's the one thing, just *one* thing that Mack and Monica and George have in common in today's world?"

I stood there thinking for a minute. Darrell said something that I didn't quite catch. "What?" I asked.

"It's something that you said about Mack. Do you remember?"

I didn't.

"*Joy?*" he said.

"I did say that, didn't I?" I said. "Yes, Mack and Monica and George certainly seemed to really be enjoying themselves. Really working hard, but enjoying themselves anyway."

"You also mentioned *passion*."

"Yeah, Mack really did have a passion for what he's doing. Everybody could tell it. Monica and George had that passion too."

"But take a look at George now," Darrell said. George was laboring through the processing of a ticket. "As you suggested, could a boss bring *joy* and *passion* by getting all over him? He might be able to make him work a little harder for a while by standing next to him with a gun pointed at his head, but could he instill *joy* and *passion*?"

"No, no, of course not," I said. "You're right. It wasn't his boss." I was thinking of my boss. He pushed me all over the park, and all I did was figure out a better way of faking it. Heck, if they gave out Academy Awards for faking it on a real job and not just in the movies, I'd have a bunch of those little statuettes on my mantel right now.

Darrell looked at his watch. "Well, time to meet George," he said.

This time I anticipated his quick departure and was walking in lockstep with him to the maintenance door. You know, you don't have to be an Einstein to pick up this time-travel stuff.

We walked through the maintenance closet and entered the newer, bustling terminal. We wove through the travelers to the food court. As we walked, a few dark clouds started to slide into my mind. I thought, *what's wrong with this picture?* Not the picture of these weird time-warp journeys, but the picture of *George*. I could understand the transformation of Mack. After all, he was on a quest to develop the best cup of coffee and the best lemon meringue pie. Heck, if he even came close, he could make a fortune. McDonald's Big Mac ain't even close to being perfect, but it paid billions to Ray Kroc.

I could also understand the transformation of Monica. She was putting together huge deals. She was on the fast track to the top of power business. But George? He could handle *at least twice as many passengers* as any other ticket agent in the world and he'd still be getting the same pay as the worst ticket agent bumbling through the day. In fact, the signs here appeared to be pointing toward a cult. You know, those people who drank the poisoned Kool-Aid believed that they were doing a beautiful thing. Now it seems we've got a genie creating a cult. I wondered if it was a two-sips-and-out deal?

George was sitting on a stool at a round table with a Wendy's double, fries and a Coke.

Darrell introduced me to George.

"Lunch," George said, pointing to his hamburger. "I start here at five-thirty in the morning."

We made some small talk about the Portland Trail Blazers, then Darrell must have sensed my mood change and decided to flame up the conversation.

"My friend here," Darrell said to George, "thinks you work too hard."

George laughed, putting down his hamburger. "I put in my eight-hour day," he said, "just like everybody else."

That was all I needed to let some of those doubting demons in my mind voice their opinions. I said, "But, you're processing at least twice as many passengers as anybody else. We were watching."

"I don't count how many people I process," George said, stuffing a french fry in his mouth. "That's almost irrelevant."

"That's not *relevant?*" I said, feeling my negative juices bubbling. Those negative juices seemed to always be simmering below the surface, but I would rarely let them out in the form of words. I'd rather just mumble to myself how stupid my boss was or how many rear ends a neighbor must have kissed to get a promotion. But today, in this goofy time-warp world, no Kool-Aid for me. "You're doing twice the work of anybody else and you're getting paid, I assume, the same? If that's not relevant, it just might be considered stupid. So, George, what *is* relevant?"

"Well, if you can ask a question like that," George said, "you're probably not going to like my answer or you probably won't understand it." George turned his head to Darrell as if he wanted to say, *Who is this stiff, anyway?*

"Explain it to me, anyway, if you can," I said.

Darrell left the table saying he was going to get us something to eat. I guess four Grand Slam breakfasts weren't enough.

"By your questions, it seems to lead to pay, to money," George said. "Well, money *is* important. Money *is* relevant. I know how much money I'm going to make. Sure, I won't make more for processing more travelers. But, *I know what I'm going to make* for a forty-hour week. To me that is important. Can I make more if I do something else for a living? Maybe. There's a lot of guys that I punch tickets for who make a lot of money. But, they're on a fast track, they take a lot of risks. I don't want the risks. I don't want the politics that it might take. So, I look to one thing."

"One thing?" I asked. This started to sound like *one wish*. Darrell returned with two single-patty hamburgers from Wendy's, two fries and two diet Cokes. He pushed one of each toward me. What was left for Darrell to eat must have looked like a starvation diet to him.

"As I was saying," George said, "the one thing I look for is to have fun."

I looked over at Darrell. He knew what I was thinking—the one wish that George made was to have fun. He answered my thoughts with a slight head shake from side to side as if to say, *Nope*.

"How can you have fun just processing tickets?" I asked.

"Well, I can see this isn't for you," George said, "and that's fine, but it's right for *me*. It isn't just the punching of the tickets, that's just something mechanical. I like to look at the bigger picture."

"The bigger picture?"

"Sure. Traveling isn't a joyride these days. Crowded airports, long lines, crowded planes, late planes, small seats, skimpy meals. If you do much of it, traveling isn't fun. So I try to make at least one small memory that *something* on the passenger's trip was pleasant. That something is me."

Very honorable, I felt like saying with striking sarcasm, but if this guy was that stupid to believe he could make a difference, I wasn't going to change him. I thought I'd challenge this idiocy in a different, less sledge-hammer approach. I said, "How can you make it a little more pleasant?"

"Do you fly much?" George asked.

"A little," I said.

"Then one of the things that must bug you is waiting in lines."

Only a genius could have said that, my demons said to me, but I just nodded.

"If you were traveling, waiting in line and you came to me, there's two things I could do for you: be nice, and process your ticket as fast as possible."

I nodded again at the genius of it all.

"The only way you notice is if I work too slow," George said. "Then it aggravates you. If I'm fast, you don't say, 'Wow, what speed you have.' But by working fast I'm not rubbing salt into a wound. To get fast, I mean really fast, I had to work on it. Most of us agents were decent typists. I, however, wanted to personally speed up the process. The best way was to take typing lessons. *Speed* typing lessons. Sure, I took typing in high school. Sixty words a minute on a manual typewriter. That was pretty good. Now I type over eighty words a minute. But speed wasn't enough. I needed more."

"A smile?" I asked, still holding down my sarcasm.

"Yes, that is important, but it's not in reference to speed. I wanted more speed than what my typing could give me. I took a basic computer class at the junior college. I didn't learn how to write programs, I learned how to write *macros*."

With macros, he explained, he was able to type in shorthand. Instead of typing fifteen keys, he could use a macro, a typing shortcut, to type five keys and get the same result. "Now that is real speed, when I use typing shortcuts so that I can actually input faster than I can physically type."

"But, what does it get you?" I asked. "It's not more pay. A promotion?"

"No, I don't get more pay," George said.

"And I'm not looking for a promotion. I've been offered promotions several times, but I'm fifty-two and I'm having fun at what I'm doing. I'm putting in the same amount of hours as a few years ago when I wasn't having any fun at all. If I'm going to have to spend about two-thirds of my waking day at work or driving to and from work, and I do have to work, I might as well have fun. I've read stuff that says you should get a job doing something that interests you. With me that's golf. Well, I think that's a crock. I really enjoy golf when I'm not working. But, I'm not good enough to be a club pro and I don't want to be a starter or marshall at some course. I enjoy being a ticket agent. It's a lot of fun for me. And, because I'm a ticket agent, I get special travel deals and I play golf all over the country."

"Well, you probably got the other agents miffed at you because it looks like you're showing them up," I said.

"They never really noticed when my typing started to improve," George said, "but once they noticed, they did sorta think I was showing them up. But then they just got used to it. I've got some good friends here."

I had to admit to myself that it was pretty

impressive that this guy went to such lengths to speed up his personal service.

"I like the Japanese part," Darrell said. "Tell him about it, George."

"There's not much to tell," George said. "It gets back to speed. We have one flight a day from Portland to Tokyo. There are quite a few Japanese travelers who aren't completely comfortable with English. They're a little hesitant because they don't want to make a mistake with our language. To speed up the process, I learned *their* language."

Learned their language? This was getting too incredible. This guy must be nuts. "Wait a minute," I said, "*you learned Japanese to speed up the process?*"

George nodded, smiling.

"How long did it take?" I asked.

"Not as long as you think," George said. "I started with a course at a junior college. I liked it, so then I took another. Then one of those mail order courses with tapes. I listened to the tapes forty-five minutes a day while commuting, for two years."

"George has made a lot of Japanese friends because of this," Darrell said.

"That's been a very rewarding, but un-anticipated benefit," George said.

Ah-so, I thought . . . there was some method behind this madness. He's got some deal going with the Japanese.

"How so?" I asked.

"Well, I've gotten to know some of the frequent travelers from Japan. When they wait in line, they'll actually let another passenger through until I'm available. That's really an honor. As you know, working for an airline, we get to travel basically for free. When I let some of these frequent Japanese travelers know that my wife and I were going to visit Japan, they couldn't have been nicer. We've visited Japan three times now and each trip I was hosted by one of my frequent travelers from Japan. They wouldn't let us buy anything. In fact, they showered us with some really nice gifts. Each trip has been a little more marvelous than the one before."

George took the last bite of his Wendy's. "I gotta get back to work. Nice meeting you," he said to me. Then he said with a wink, "I hope you wish for the right thing. I did and I've never been a happier man."

After George left, Darrell said, "That's a

pretty good example of E-W-E. You see, to have a great E-W-E, you don't have to put in longer hours. Heck, George just puts in his eight hours a day just like anybody else there. But, he has a highly *Effective Work Ethic.*"

Darrell slurped down the rest of his Coke and then asked me, "Do you consider George successful?"

"Successful?"

"Yes, successful."

"Well, I guess it all depends on what you use as the benchmarks for measuring success. If it's money, no, he's not particularly successful."

"Is money the only benchmark?" Darrell asked.

"It's an important one," I said.

"If it is, then what about a great social worker? Or a great anthropologist? What about a great third grade teacher? Using money as the benchmark, they would each be considered *un*successful. *Failures.* I think money probably isn't that important to them. Mack and George would certainly be unsuccessful in that framework, but look at them . . . could you say that they were unsuccessful? Do you think they *feel* unsuccessful?"

I had seen Mack and George at work. They had the joy of achieving, the passion for work, even if it was a little bit weird. Monica clearly made more money, but she didn't look stressed out, tight, ready to bust a capillary. She had that same joy and passion Mack and George had. A *joy* and a *passion* that I had never known. And, if the benchmark for success did include money, then I've never known that either.

But, they did indeed have *joy* and they did indeed have *passion*. How much money would I pay for having *joy* and *passion* on a job? Such an absurd idea. I don't even know the price tag.

Chapter 7

"Let's go," Darrell said, crumbling up the hamburger wrappings and putting them in the trash can.

We walked to my car. I got behind the wheel. "Where to now?" I asked.

"Your office, pal," Darrell said. "I've taken up enough of your time today. You have to get to work."

As we approached my office building in suburban Beaverton, I noticed the sun was lower than it should have been. It was about noon, but the sun was on the eastern horizon. I looked at my watch. 11:49 A.M. Just as I was going to glance away from my watch, I noticed the minute hand start to move *backwards*. It started reversing slowly, about one minute per second. Then it picked up steam and it circled the face of the watch in about ten seconds. My watch had lost an hour in about ten seconds! The next hour was lost in about five seconds. I stared at it, the minute hand flying backwards in a blur, and it came to a stop at 9:31 A.M.

"Neat trick, eh?" Darrell said. "How time flies! Backwards!"

Why should I be surprised? We had walked through mirrors and maintenance closets traversing time. Now we did it just sitting in my car.

"You'll find this interesting," Darrell said, as he got out of my car. I had parked it in my usual spot in the parking lot behind my office.

We walked inside. You could smell coffee. A number of other real estate agents were at their cubicles making phone calls. I mumbled my usual hello as we walked through, but they seemed to be involved in their phone conversations and didn't acknowledge me. As I walked to my cubicle, I saw the boss in his office on the phone. I waved, but he didn't see me. I turned the corner to my cubicle, and saw that I was *already* there.

I stopped abruptly. I was already sitting

at my desk, reading the sports section of *The Oregonian.*

I turned and looked at Darrell.

"I thought you'd like to see what *you* look like," he said, "at work."

"We're invisible?" I asked, catching on even more to this time-warp stuff.

He nodded.

I walked over to one of my co-workers. "I've got that twenty dollars that I owe you," I said to the salesman in the next cubicle. I waved a twenty-dollar bill out to him as if it were a small flag. He didn't look up. He didn't grab it. That might have been his only chance to get it back. Tough luck for him.

This invisible stuff was getting to be a little fun. I walked over to my boss's office. He was just hanging up the phone. "Hey, Jerry," I said, "before you make another call, let me ask you a question. Did you know you're a jerk?"

No response.

Darrell came up behind me. "I wouldn't push it," he said. "This time travel isn't an exact science, you know. Sometimes parts of different worlds overlap, at least in a person's memory."

I backed away. Darrell said, "C'mon, let's you and me watch *you*. You might find it very interesting."

We walked back to my cubicle.

I don't know what is more boring. Living my life or watching my life. While others were answering phones, writing things on memo pads, or looking through the multiple listing book, I just sat there reading the paper. My only activity was getting up to refill my coffee.

Finally, the phone rang. I watched myself pick it up. Almost as a reflex action, I saw my feet elevate to the desk. Yep, that was my usual position, all right. Feet up on my desk while I was on the phone. A real big-shot.

As if to justify myself to Darrell, I said, "Well, what can I say, it's a boring job."

"More boring than making coffee and serving lemon meringue pie all day?" he said. "Or punching tickets?"

I remembered seeing Mack and George working with so much joy and passion. Then I remembered when we walked through the time warp and saw them looking like me. Bored, sleepy, waiting for something to happen. That was *me*. I wondered *how many years* people like

Mack, George and me would be waiting for something to happen.

My real life was boring enough, but watching it was even worse. It was fun watching Mack and George when they had that joy and passion for working. And, it had looked like they were having *fun* at work.

I guess I never equated *fun* and *work*. Work was something you *had* to do. Sort of like when we were kids and we *had* to go to school. It wasn't optional. Sure, school, like work, had elements of fun. The camaraderie of school was fun. I remember that recess was fun in grade school. Sometimes there was a certain camaraderie at work that was fun. But, I equated work to taking a history class. What fun is that?

"How long do we have to watch this?" I asked Darrell.

"Well, we could walk through that closet door and go into your past about five years ago. Would that be any more exciting?"

I physically shuddered. "The only thing that would change would be the date on the newspaper," I said. It's not that I was lazy. I put in at least forty hours a week. Probably closer to fifty when you consider the weekends showing houses to people who seemed to just want to look. However, I just might be 'Exhibit B' on E-W-E, *Effective* Work Ethic. I put in my time, a lot of time. It's just not always very effective.

Instead of going back about five years, a better idea came to me. "Hey, Darrell, let's take a peek at the future."

"I normally don't go into the future," Darrell said.

"Why not?"

"Don't need to," Darrell said. "You've seen the present with Mack and Monica and George. And, you've seen their past. Is there any doubt that their future will be even more fun and exciting?"

He had a point. Mack and Monica and George weren't going to lose their joy and passion for work.

"But, with you, I'll make an exception," Darrell said. "Wanna go to the future, pal, we'll go."

"Let's go," I said.

"Follow me," Darrell said. He headed for the room that had the copying machine, the coffee machine and reams of paper.

Darrell helped himself to the coffee. "You

got any real cream or just this junk?" Darrell asked, pointing to the powdered cream. I told him the powdered stuff was it.

"Any bagels? Donuts?"

"Nope, you got to bring your own."

"OK, let's go take a look at the future," Darrell said, grumbling as if he had to make the journey on an empty stomach. He walked around me to the office.

I followed him back to my cubicle. I was sitting there reading *The Oregonian* sports section.

"C'mon, Darrell," I said, "you trying to pull a practical joke or something? Nothing has changed. We haven't walked five years into the future."

"Take a look at the newspaper, pal."

I picked up the front section of *The Oregonian*. Damnation! It was *five years* from just a few minutes ago. Nothing had changed except time. I took a closer look at me. The me sitting at my cubicle was developing a paunch. A few gray hairs too. And, jeez, my hair was thinning pretty good on the back top of my head. When my future me turned the page of the paper, I noticed that I no longer had a wedding ring on my finger. I glanced over at the corner of my desk. My wife's picture was gone. It wasn't replaced by any alluring actress type. There was just an empty space.

"What about the wish?" I asked Darrell.

"What about it?"

"I thought that with that one wish, things would have changed, like it did for Mack and Monica and George," I said. "Heck, this is as boring as five years ago."

"You wished for the wrong thing."

Chapter 8

"*Wished for the wrong thing?*" I practically shouted.

Darrell nodded.

"*How is that possible?*" I demanded. I was still hyper. Here's the one chance—albeit as illogical as it can be, coming from a genie—to hit The Big One and *nothing had changed.* It was akin to being able to buy Microsoft stock in 1980 for a few pennies and declining because you'd thought that Bill Gates and Paul Allen were just a couple of propeller-heads who wouldn't amount to anything.

"You were supposed to *guide* me, to *help* me," I said.

"Well, first of all, there is no rule that I

have to guide you or help you. I'm like a mail-man. I just deliver, I don't write the letter," Darrell said. "But, I believe in a more personal service so I *have* guided you. I have shown you Mack before and after his wish. I have shown you Monica before and after her wish. I have shown you George before and after his wish. And finally, I have shown you *yourself* before and after *your* wish. You just didn't pay attention. You simply made the wrong wish, pal."

"What did I wish for?"

"You'll find out," Darrell said. "But, remember, I'm a genie and in your case I can grant you one wish under the ground rules that empower me. I don't come here and say, '*Hey, pal, here's your wish.*' You've got a free choice, a free will in this. *The choice is all yours.* You can't blame me for your wish . . . or for your life."

I looked back at myself reading the paper. I sat down on the spare plastic chair alongside my cubicle. I was just a couple of feet from my future self. This was what I had to look forward to? Just more of what I had been living? Actually, a little *less* than what I had been living. My wife was gone. I don't think she had died; if she had, I probably would have kept her picture on my desk. No, she left me. Sure, things weren't that terrific between us all of the time, but it wasn't *that bad*. It's not like George Costanza's parents were on *Seinfeld*.

"If you could see yourself now," I said to my future self, "you'd put down that stupid paper and do something."

My future self just sat there reading the paper.

"You're just taking up space!" I yelled.

My future self just sat there reading the paper.

I was about to get up when a man walked over to my future self. It was a guy who I didn't recognize. He had probably been hired within the past five years. He looked to be in his early sixties.

"I got a mailing from Social Security," the man said. "I might be able to pull the trigger and retire at sixty-two. I don't know, though."

"Well, if it was me," my future self said, "I'd pull the trigger. I think about that every day."

"You do?" the man said. "You're in your early forties. You have twenty years to go."

"Twenty years and counting," my future

self said. "Even now, I've done some figuring. I think I could live on the benefits; then it's no more of this crap every day."

"What would you do?" the man said.

"Nothing. Play a little golf, go to a few Minor League baseball games, fish. Maybe travel a bit."

"Well, you've got twenty years to think about it," he said.

"Every day, every day," my future self said, as if it were some terrific erotic and exotic thought.

I got up from the plastic chair and walked toward Darrell. I took a look back at my future self. "Idiot," I said, and turned to walk out of the office.

Darrell joined me outside.

"Where to now?" I asked him. I then noticed that the cars in the parking lot looked different. Not a *lot* different, but the designs of the cars were a little different. Parked in the space where I would normally park my Ford Taurus was a Porsche. Who was the jerk that parked in my parking spot?! I walked over to it and looked inside.

In the little backseat I recognized my golf clubs. The car hadn't been washed for quite a while and there was a ding on the left front fender. Some of the paint had chipped off and rust had formed.

I turned to Darrell. "This is still five years into the future, isn't it?"

Darrell nodded.

"This Porsche, it's mine?"

Darrell nodded.

It gave me hope. Maybe things had turned up, maybe I had wished for the right thing and this was one of the fruits of my new life. Maybe, *just maybe*, the future self I saw was only a brief snapshot that wasn't really indicative of the way I lived. Yeah, maybe I wasn't married anymore, but with this Porsche maybe I had some beautiful young thing instead.

Then an awful thought struck me.

"*This* isn't what I wished for, is it?" I asked Darrell.

He nodded.

"*NOOOOOOOOOO!*" I screamed. "I couldn't have been this stupid! Get one wish from a genie and *I wish for a Porsche?*"

Chapter 9

I was driving now. Not the Porsche, but my Ford Taurus. Darrell was in the passenger seat.

We had re-entered my office, walked by the coffee machine and then walked out again into the parking lot. We time-traveled back to the present. Amazing how easy this time-travel stuff is if you know the tricks.

I felt like speeding up and driving the car into a brick wall. How stupid I was. A *Porsche*! Instead of speeding up, I slowed down. I turned into a parking space in front of a seedy-looking bar.

I had never been to this bar before. I had driven by it enough times, but it looked like a real big-time drinkers bar.

Inside, it was dimly lit. There were four or five guys at the bar. It looked like they were in for the duration of the day. There were a few small tables with chairs. These were empty. No eaters here, just slap down a twenty-dollar bill on the bar and keep drinking until the twenty is gone. Then, perhaps, fish out another twenty-dollar bill and do it again.

We walked over to an empty corner table and sat down. The waitress took our orders. A Scotch on the rocks for me. A diet Coke for Darrell.

As she was placing the drinks in front of us, I said to the waitress, "I'll have another one of those."

She nodded. She had seen the type before.

I slurped down the Scotch like I was drinking Gatorade after playing a round of tennis.

The waitress was good. The second Scotch was there in a blink. I nodded to her for another. She gave me a slight nod back. Yes, she had seen the type and knew how to provide the quick drinks.

"All I've ever wanted is to be happy," I

said to Darrell. "Just like anybody else, only wanted to be happy."

Darrell took a sip of his diet Coke.

"You know, Darrell," I said, "they should have classes in how to be happy. They should have taught us that in school."

"Like the three r's—readin', 'ritin' and 'rithmetic?" Darrell said.

"Well, yes. Otherwise the only way we learn how to be happy is watching *Gilligan's Island* or *Leave It to Beaver* or *Captain Kangaroo*. How stupid is that?"

"Well, now you don't have to watch *Gilligan's Island*, wherever that is," Darrell said. "You got me instead, and one wish. So what's the one wish gonna be, pal? To be happy?"

"Yes! That would be everybody's wish, wouldn't it?"

"I can grant you that wish," Darrell said. "To be happy."

He fished into his suit pocket and brought out a set of car keys. He tossed them on the table.

The familiar Porsche crest was on the key chain.

"Here's happiness," Darrell said.

I picked up the keys. It surprised me, but

I felt a strange surge of power emanating from the keys. I downed the rest of my third Scotch. This stuff wasn't affecting me at all. They must serve watered-down drinks. I chewed on the ice.

When you think about a Porsche and fondle the keys, you do feel a certain power, a certain type of happiness. A Porsche was a statement of success, something that I had always been looking for.

I thought about how the Porsche could change my life. When I took a customer to look at a house, the customer would be impressed. The customer would think that he was dealing with a highly successful real estate agent. The customer would listen more carefully to what I said. I'd close more deals. It would have a positive effect on my wife, too. She'd see a different me. She'd sense that I was more important. She'd cheerlead me as I closed deal after deal after deal. Yes, as stupid as it seemed back at my office, maybe the Porsche would jump-start me, maybe a Porsche was the *right* wish. Yes, this was an auspicious train of thought.

A moment of clear thinking washed across me. *Wait just a minute!* Am I now making the stupid decision that I had just minutes ago cursed myself for? I was! I was luring myself into taking a Porsche as my wish. Maybe when I had made the decision before, I had been drinking. Wow, these parallel worlds can get confusing. Yes, the Porsche would make me happy. Short-term. Maybe a month. But, it wouldn't really change anything. I pushed the car keys across the table toward Darrell.

"Those keys would provide me short-term happiness, Darrell," I said, "but I've pursued short-term happiness all my life. I'm an expert on that. I want long-term happiness. I want happiness for the rest of my life."

"That's your 'official' wish?" Darrell asked.

"Yes," I said, almost with a posture of defiance. "*Yes*, that's what my *official* wish is. *I want happiness for the rest of my life.*"

"That's your one wish?" Darrell asked again.

"Yes, yes, yes," I said. "That's it, pal." I added the 'pal' to mimic Darrell a little.

"I can do that," Darrell said. "Sure, I can do that."

"Well, what do we do next? Do you zap me or something?"

"I need to give you a warning first," Darrell said.

"Uh-oh, here we go," I said. "More ground rules."

"No, no, it's nothing like that. I just wanted to be able to explain happiness to you. If you had taken those Porsche keys, you would have been happy, right?"

"Right."

"But, what happens if you hadn't taken care of the car?"

"How so?" I asked.

"You know, oil changes, lube jobs, tune-ups, those types of things. What if you did *none* of those things? The performance of the Porsche would have gotten worse and worse. After a while, you'd be really unhappy about that car."

"I wouldn't do that," I said. "That would be stupid. I'd give it oil changes, I'd get it tuned. I'd take care of it."

"Oh, you would, would you?" Darrell said. "If we went back to the parking lot and took a test spin of that Porsche with your golf clubs in the backseat, you'd find that your Ford Taurus performed much better than your Porsche. You'd find that your Porsche badly needed a tune-up, but you didn't want to spend the four hundred dollars it cost to get one. What about the left front fender. Yeah, dings will happen. But you saw the rust. That ding has been there for a while. You didn't have it fixed. You're driving a five-year-old car that's closing in on becoming an old piece of junk, pal, and you started out with one of the finest cars money can buy. The same thing applies to happiness. If you don't take care of it, if you don't provide the 'oil changes and lube jobs and tune-ups,' then happiness turns pretty quickly into a clunker."

"So how do you take happiness in for a tune-up?" I asked.

"Well, that's what *you* have to provide to support your wish," Darrell said. "The oil changes, the lube jobs, the tune-ups. You've *already* got the Porsche. The Porsche is *you*. Whether you have thought about it or not, like a Porsche, you're a wonderful machine. Far better than what those German auto guys could have created. What you've needed is the oil changes, lube jobs and tune-ups. I can't grant you those. *You* gotta provide them. If you provide them, you'll be just like a finely tuned race car."

"OK," I said. "I'm getting tired of talking

about analogies—just what *are* those so-called 'oil changes, lube jobs and tune-ups' that I gotta provide? I'm ready."

"Not so fast," Darrell said. "The first step to happiness is that you have to change your thinking a little bit. Not a lot, just a little bit. You'll be able to do it easily."

"What do I have to do?"

"Don't think 'happiness.' Don't even *think* it. Think *'success in what you do for a living,'*" Darrell said. "That's the first step and a small one at that. *Think success in what you do for a living.* Happiness is a by-product of being successful."

Darrell held up his hand as if to stop me from talking. You bet I was going to debate what he was saying.

"I know what you're going to say," Darrell said, "that there are a lot of what you consider successful people who really aren't happy. They've got broken marriages. They've got alcohol problems. They got *problems*."

"Right!"

"Let's first take an opposite look at the premise," Darrell said. "I said, 'Happiness is a by-product of being successful.' Here's the opposite: Can you be happy if you're not successful?"

I thought about that for a moment. Can you be happy if you're not successful? *Can you be happy if you're not successful?*

Before I could say anything, Darrell said, "For instance, let's say you're a third grade teacher. You hate your job. You hate the kids you are teaching. You hate the kids' parents. You really don't like many of your fellow teachers. As if it were a great surprise, you're also a lousy teacher. You just couldn't be a great teacher if you hated your job, hated the kids, hated your fellow teachers. Now, and this is important, *could that third grade teacher be happy in the other parts of his or her life?* Could that teacher have a satisfying marriage? Of course not.

"That third grade teacher would be just as unhappy off the job as on the job. Sure, that teacher might be able to drown his or her unhappiness with TV or some inane hobby or even with drinking, but no matter what, that teacher would be unhappy.

"Look at the reverse. What if that third grade teacher loved the job, loved the students, loved the challenge, liked the fellow teachers? Most likely that teacher would be a great teacher. And would be considered successful at what he or she does for a living. My feeling is, that third grade teacher would have a better marriage, be more involved in the other parts of his or her life. In short, that teacher would be *happy*."

How could I argue with that? I could throw money into the equation. As we all know, third grade teachers don't make a fortune. "What about money?" I asked.

"That's where people confuse the issue," Darrell said. "Yeah, yeah, yeah, we've all heard that money doesn't buy happiness. Well, let's look at what *does* buy happiness. If money isn't it, *what does buy happiness?*"

I shrugged my shoulders.

Darrell hunched over the table. He was really into it. He said, "What buys happiness for third grade teachers is that they *love their jobs*, they love their students, they love the challenge of accelerating the progress of their students."

"They have a joy and a passion for their work like Mack and Monica and George," I said.

"That's right, they have a *joy* and a *passion* in *what they do for a living*. If they had a little more money, that would be terrific because they'd be able to buy a few more things, but that wouldn't make them any more happy. Look at George. George really can't make any more money. But does he seem happy?"

"He sure does. I'd love to feel the way he feels," I said.

"That's what the oil changes, lube jobs and tune-ups do," Darrell said. "Once you start thinking *success at what you do for a living*, then you just need to apply the oil changes, lube jobs and tune-ups. It works automatically, positively, every time, no matter if you're a real estate salesman or a third grade teacher or an anthropologist or a ticket agent or a farmer or a heart surgeon. *It works automatically, positively, every time, for everybody.* It absolutely, positively cannot fail. You see those stiffs over at the bar? It would work automatically, positively, every time for them too."

"Well, then tell me what those oil changes, lube jobs and tune-ups are," I said.

"Not here," Darrell said. "Let's get out of

this dive." Darrell looked at the check on the corner of the table. He reached into his pocket and dropped a bunch of bills on the table. "My treat," he said, and walked out of the bar.

Chapter 10

Darrell took the keys from me. "Designated driver," he said. "This time you really need it. I know a place where we can get a great cup of coffee and a great piece of lemon meringue pie. That'll help sober you up."

The drive to Mack's Diner took only about five minutes. Strange, it had only taken a few minutes when we were coming back from the beach, over an hour away from here. The way this time-travel stuff was set up, Mack's one diner was more convenient than the thousands of McDonald's.

We walked into the diner. It was full of people. Toward the back, I saw somebody waving at us. It was George, the ticket agent at the airport. He was sitting with Monica, the stock-broker. We walked over to their table. In front of each was a partly eaten piece of lemon meringue pie and a cup of coffee.

"Join us," George said. We sat down. Mack came over with three cups and a pot of coffee. He set down the cups, poured coffee into each and put cups in front of Darrell and me. The aroma was terrific! Mack then pulled over an empty chair from a nearby table.

"I'm taking a break," Mack said. "Marie will take care of the customers." He then turned to me and said, "Good to see you again."

"Go ahead and tell them," Darrell said.

"Tell them what?" I said.

"Tell them that you're ready to make your wish."

"I am?"

"You were about ten minutes ago," Darrell said. "Remember the Porsche?"

"You were going to choose a *Porsche*?" George asked.

I nodded and then shrugged my shoulders as if that would somehow explain my temporary insanity.

As I was shrugging helplessly, Marie

delivered three pieces of lemon meringue pie. Great timing!

With a mouth full of lemon meringue pie, I felt I could explain further. "Well, sort of," I said. "I was just *thinking* about it, about a Porsche—I had had a couple of drinks. It wasn't an *official* wish. Darrell suggested I should instead '*think success in what I do for a living.*' "

"Good advice," Monica said, taking a bite from her piece of pie.

"Yes, very good advice," Mack said. "By the way, can you taste the difference in the lemons? I had them flown in from Israel today. No—don't worry about that; just enjoy."

"Darrell was going to tell me about oil changes, lube jobs and tune-ups," I said.

George, Monica and Mack all chuckled as if it was an insiders' joke.

"He said that oil changes, lube jobs and tune-ups work absolutely, positively every time for everybody, that it is absolutely, positively impossible for them to fail," I said. "Can I ask you guys, what was your oil change?"

"Easy," said Mack, "I cleaned up my kitchen. I steam cleaned it, scrubbed it, washed it, polished it. I made it look brand new."

"I took some typing lessons," George said. "I went from typing about sixty words a minute to over eighty words a minute."

"I took a Dale Carnegie class," Monica said. "You know, where you have to get up in front of strangers and give a little speech."

"Those are *oil changes*?"

"Oil changes in our careers," Mack said. "We had all that crummy oil in the system. The oil change was to *improve something*."

"Improve something? *That's it?*" I asked.

"It does sound mundane," Mack said. "On the surface, cleaning the kitchen *sounds* like just a maintenance job. And it is just that. It's something I should have been doing regularly. What was important about it was that it was *part of something*. It wasn't just an isolated cleaning exercise."

"The same with my typing lessons," George said. "On the surface, typing lessons were nice, but I didn't really need them. I could type decently. But, it was *part of something*."

"And the same with my attending Dale Carnegie," Monica said. "On the surface, it sounds good that I took the course, although I wasn't a shrinking violet before I took it. But, it was *part of something*."

"What was the something it was part of?" I asked.

"Every ninety days," George said.

"Yep, every ninety days," Mack said.

"Every ninety days," Monica said.

"What do you mean 'every ninety days'?" I asked.

"If you want to *think success in what you do for a living,*" Mack said, "*you must* provide the oil changes, lube jobs and tune-ups."

"That means improve or initiate up to three things every ninety days," George said.

"That's it?" I asked. "*Improve or initiate up to three things every ninety days?*"

All three nodded their heads.

"That's a little simplistic, isn't it?" I asked.

"Yes, it *sounds* simplistic," Monica said. "But, if you think it through, it isn't simplistic at all. You could say that people are improving and initiating something new all the time. But that's only partly true. Improving or initiating something new, for most people, is usually *random* and *infrequent* and often *unplanned*. What we're talking about is *not random*, it's *not infrequent*, it's *not unplanned*."

115

"Why just three things?" I asked.

"*Up to* three things," George corrected me. "It could be only one thing that you would try to improve or initiate. If you made a list of things to improve or initiate, it could have a dozen or more items. That's too many. You'd be overwhelmed. Your actions would become paralyzed. *Up to* three things is not too many, you can focus."

"Also, it makes *you* make a decision," Mack said. "*You* have to decide what the three things are. It's not your boss, it's not your spouse, it's not your parents. It's *you*. If *you* are making the decision and choosing up to three things, you find that you have a little more dedication, a little more vigor in improving or initiating. Now you can see how it's planned and not random."

Mack nodded to Marie, the waitress. Since we had all finished our pieces of lemon meringue pie, she was bringing over another serving. Normally, I'm not a big fan of desserts. But this pie was the best.

Mack continued, "I'll give you an example of me choosing. My first 'oil change' was to clean the kitchen. That improved something that I do for a living. However, if somebody had *told* me that I *had* to clean up the kitchen, I probably would have done it, but not with the dedication and vigor it took to make it amazingly spotless."

That made sense to me. My boss had stopped trying to suggest areas for me to improve after he saw how I had either resisted his suggestions or just gone through the motions.

"*You* get to choose what you want to improve," Monica said. "After meeting Darrell, I started to *think* that I could make the move from secretary to broker. I had done most of the prep work for my boss anyway. Now I would do that same work for myself, and close the deals by myself. But I lacked self-confidence in making that move. I took the Dale Carnegie course just to improve my confidence. If my boss had suggested taking the course, I probably would have thought, *What's with him?*"

"*You* also get to choose *how much* you want to improve or *how far* to take a new project," George said. "*You* set the benchmarks. For instance, when I started taking typing lessons, I was thinking that I wanted to reach a hundred words a minute. Someplace along the line *I* decided that eighty words a minute was enough.

After all, I wasn't typing long documents. With what I was typing every day, eighty words a minute had the effect of doubling my efficiency. Reaching a hundred words a minute wouldn't have provided any more efficiency. So, what did I do? I stopped taking lessons. I dropped out of that class. If *somebody else* had set my goals, I would have continued on without purpose. I probably would have gotten bored. I might have even resented it. I wouldn't have been as eager to start improving something else."

That also made sense to me. A lot of sense.

"Yeah, look at my coffee," Mack said. "I just wanted to improve it a bit. It was so awful before—"

"You can say that again," Darrell interrupted. He had just been listening, nodding his head.

Mack laughed. "Well, I just wanted to focus on the coffee as one of my three improvements in ninety days. But then I really got into it. It no longer became something I wanted to improve. It sorta crossed over into the category of *initiating something new*. I spent hours buying exotic coffee beans, experimenting, tasting.

It became *fun*. I was initiating something new. Each day I could hardly wait to get to the diner to see how my customers liked my new blend."

"That's when I started to notice a joy of work, a passion in Mack," Darrell said. "As you saw for yourself," he said to me, "that joy and passion are unmistakable—they just exude from a person."

"And it doesn't go away," George said, "as long as you're improving or initiating up to three things every ninety days. You see, whether you realize it or not at the time, *you're completely reshaping your job*, no matter what it is, into what *you* want that job to be."

"Yeah," Mack said, "look at George's job. It's punching tickets. You can't get away from that. But boy, does he have fun."

"The reason I have fun," George said, "is that I am improving or initiating something new in *everything around* punching the tickets. I've reshaped that job to *what I wanted it to be*."

"Why every ninety days?" I asked.

"It's like a corporation's Quarterly Report," Darrell said, "except we look at it as a Quarterly *Preview*. A corporation's Quarterly Report is basically a report card on how they performed over the past ninety days. A Quarterly *Preview* is a conscious, planned effort to look at how to improve over the *next* ninety days. Ninety days is enough time to improve something or to initiate something. And, there are four ninety-day segments in a year. That's breaking the year up into bite-size pieces. Now you've got four Quarterly Previews in each year."

"Think this through for a minute," George said. "Let's say you came up with three things that you wanted to improve or initiate every ninety days. That would be *twelve things* that you initiated or improved in one year! Just think how your job would have changed! *You would have completely reshaped your job the way you would want it to be.* Sure, the basic function may be the same—like punching tickets for me—but everything around that job function would have changed. You would've reshaped that job the way *you* wanted it to be. If you were with a big corporation, your boss would notice your improvement, or your boss's boss would notice it. You'd probably get promotions a lot faster, you'd be on a fast track. Take a look at Monica. She's on a real fast track and people upstairs notice her improvement. One day she'll be running the whole joint."

"Let's look at it more conservatively," Monica said. "What if you could come up with *only one thing* to improve or initiate every ninety days? Just one. That would be four things that you would improve or initiate in one year. Think how those four things could change your job!"

"In two years, you could have improved or initiated eight to twenty-four things," Darrell said. "And when you look at it in ninety-day bites, it's not too intimidating."

"In fact, it's pretty easy," Mack said.

"The most difficult part isn't improving or initiating," Monica said. "You'll find that after a while the most difficult part is the *planning*. Yeah, sure, in the first few ninety-day segments, it's relatively easy to figure out what to improve or initiate. For instance, can I ask you, what one thing would you like to improve or initiate over the next ninety days?"

That wasn't a difficult question at all. I took a sip of that wonderful coffee. "Well, one thing that I would like to improve," I said, "is to come in earlier to work. Instead of coming in at nine-thirty in the morning, I'd like to come in about eight o'clock. I'd probably be the first one in the office at that time."

"See how easy it was to come up with that first thing?" Monica said. "Now, what's the degree of difficulty to be the first one in the office?"

"Not difficult at all," I said. "I get up at five-thirty on the weekends to play golf. It's not difficult to get to work early. I just don't know what I'd do there that early. Except maybe read the paper earlier."

"Don't worry about what you would do if you got there at eight o'clock," Darrell said. "If you decide to improve or initiate something else, you've now created the time for that. In fact, you would have an extra hour and a half every day—or *seven and a half hours a week*—to work on that other thing to improve or initiate. That's like getting an extra day a week."

"Now, what would you like to improve or initiate once you've found an extra day a week?" George asked.

I took another sip of coffee. I ate another bite of the pie.

"You see," Mack said, "the first thing to

improve or initiate came really easy. Now you're having to *think*. That's good. Nobody's *telling* you what you gotta do. You're *planning* it."

"Yeah, I like this," I said. "You know, with that extra time, there is one thing I'd like to initiate. I've been thinking about it off and on for a while, but I just keep putting it off."

"What's that?"

"Well, let me bore you a little bit about the residential real estate business," I said. "A key to this business is to get referrals. You know—to get people I know to recommend to friends who are looking to sell their houses to use me as the listing agent. If I'm the listing agent, I get fifty percent of the commission no matter who sells the house."

"How many real estate agents are there in the Portland area?" George asked.

"About six thousand," I said.

"Wow. If you were the listing agent," George said, "you'd have potentially six thousand real estate agents trying to sell the house you listed. Yes, I can see where it is important to be the listing agent."

"And, if *I* sell the house that I listed," I

said, "I get all of the commission. So, I've been thinking about how to increase my listings. People always know *somebody* who is thinking about selling their house. I just have to have them think of me. But, you can't always be bugging your friends, saying, 'Know anybody who wants to sell their house?' After a while, you wouldn't have any friends."

"So how do you get them to think about you?" Monica asked.

"A greeting card," I said. "Not a birthday card. But a humorous *Listing Card*. In a light, humorous way, I'd send a card out about every . . . well . . . ninety days to all my friends and acquaintances. People like getting cards. They'd enjoy mine, and some of them would recommend me to a person who is thinking about selling their house."

"Good idea," George said. "Who makes these cards?"

"Nobody," I said. "I've been thinking about creating my own. I think I could do it on a computer. There's only one problem and that's made me procrastinate on it."

"What's that?" Mack asked.

"I don't know how to work a computer."

"Aha . . . there's the *second thing* that you can improve or initiate," George said. "You've got an extra hour and a half each day to learn, really learn the computer. Graphic programs are so much easier to learn today. You'll learn these so fast that you'll amaze even yourself."

"Right, *right!*" I said. It was like a light-bulb had been turned on in my head. "I really hadn't been thinking about it that way."

"OK, that's all," Darrell said. "You've got three things to improve or initiate over the next ninety days. *One*, get into the office at eight o'clock every day. *Two*, take a computer class. *Three*, create the first one of those Listing Greeting Cards. Write those down. Don't write down any more. Just concentrate on those three. Don't even *think* about what your three things will be in the ninety-day period following this ninety days. Just think about these three things for the next ninety days."

"Do you see how they sort of flow together," Monica said, "when you're thinking about how to be successful in what you do for a living? *One thing just naturally leads to another.* The key is *you* choosing how you want to shape your job."

"Not to put a negative spin on this," Darrell said, "but what would be the consequences if the Listing Greeting Card thing didn't work out?"

I thought about that for a moment. What if this idea didn't work at getting any listings? What if I just sent out a bunch of cute cards and nothing happened?

"Well, at least I would know that I gave it a good shot," I said.

"*And* you made it a habit of being the first one in the office *and* you learned the computer," Darrell said. "With that new habit and that new skill, you would be better prepared to improve or initiate things in your *next* ninety days. And once you're on the track to improve or initiate up to three things every ninety days, you'll find that *improvement begets improvement*, that *initiating new things begets initiating new things*."

"You've probably got a better idea now of E-W-E—Effective Work Ethic—don't you?" asked Mack.

"I sure do—improving and initiating up to three things every ninety days," I said. "I'm getting excited. I can see why you guys have so much joy and passion in your jobs. I'm starting to feel more joy and passion for *my* job than ever before, and I haven't even started E-W-E yet!"

I took another sip of coffee. It was time for me to officially make the wish. "OK, how do I do this—how do I make the wish?" I asked.

Darrell laughed. "Just like when you were a little kid," Darrell said, "except you don't have to close your eyes and blow out any candles. And unlike Dorothy in *The Wizard of Oz*, you don't have to click your heels together three times. Just state your wish."

I cleared my throat a little. "*I wish for success in what I do for a living*," I said.

There were no lightning bolts. No thunder. No drumroll. No fireworks. It was just like I was talking. Darrell should add some special effects.

"I grant you the wish," Darrell said.

"That's it? That's all there is to it?" I asked.

"That's all there is to it," Darrell said.

"Let him make an amendment to that," Mack said.

Darrell looked at Mack questioningly.

"Let him add 'joy and passion for doing—'" Mack said.

"That's a qualifying phrase that isn't necessary," Darrell said. "What he wished for, *'I wish for success in what I do for a living,'* is ample. If he provides the oil changes, lube jobs and tune-ups, the joy and passion for doing his job will just naturally happen. The *only* way to have joy and passion in work is to improve or initiate things. Once you stop improving or initiating, it gets boring. I've granted him his wish, now it's up to him to care for it."

Mack, Monica and George congratulated me.

"You're going to have the time of your life," Mack said.

"You'll see," George said. "You're going to have so much fun, so much fun." George looked at his watch. "Well, I think I've had *my* quota of lemon meringue pie, but my wife hasn't. Mack, can I get a piece to go?"

"Sure, George, follow me. I've got to get back to work anyway," Mack said.

"And I've got a plane to catch," Monica said.

Mack, Monica and George shook my hand, congratulated me again, and Darrell and I were left alone.

"What's next?" I asked Darrell.

"You go to work tomorrow at eight o'clock, that's what's next," Darrell said.

He got up from the table.

"Oh, there is one more thing," Darrell said. "You've got to insert me in another receptacle. It can't be a spray can. I should've never let that guy put me in there. Jeez, the can falls into the ocean and I gotta travel seven thousand miles. Some of those waves on the Pacific get pretty big, you know. Plus, it might have been decades before somebody found me. Think of all those wishes that wouldn't have been made 'cause I was sitting in some spray paint can in the middle of the ocean or on some desolate beach. What a waste that would have been."

"So, how do we do this?" I asked.

"Follow me, pal," Darrell said.

Haven't I always, I thought.

We left the diner and walked across the street. I wasn't familiar with this street. It sure wasn't the road to the Oregon beaches where Mack's Diner was located before.

We walked to a gas station. It was busy with cars being attended to. There was a soda machine against the side of the building.

"Right here," Darrell said, pointing to the soda machine.

"Right here? How do we do this?"

"Just pick a flavor," Darrell said. "Point to one."

"That's it?"

"That's it," Darrell said. "I'll be checking in with you occasionally, just like I do with Mack, George and Monica. Well, my friend, you are now positioned to *ride the right horse*, you. But you gotta ride it. You gotta use the oil changes, lube jobs and tune-ups. You've seen the future if you don't. So, as they used to say in those old cowboy movies, *let's ride!*

"OK, pal, what flavor do you like?"

I pointed to a cola drink. Diet.

In a swoosh and a flash almost like a mini-tornado, Darrell flew into the can. The top was never popped. Just somehow, some way, Darrell was now in that sealed diet cola can.

Wow, what a great special effect!

I walked back across the street to my car. I got in, started it and pulled out on the road. The road, thanks to time travel, was now the familiar road that led to my house.

As I drove home, I was thinking over the

whole experience. It seemed so crazy. So unbelievable. Yes, there are some things in life that are impossible to explain without somebody thinking you're crazy. This is probably one of them. And yet, I had been given this one opportunity to be successful in what I do for a living. And be happy. To have a meaningful marriage. So how crazy is that?

As I drove, a thought made me start to chuckle. The chuckle led to a laugh. I was laughing out loud as I drove. It was the thought of some weary person pulling in to get gas. Getting out of the car. Fishing into his or her pocket for four quarters for the soda machine. Picking a diet cola. And yes, this unsuspecting person pulling the tab on the can. And then *vrooooom*, their life will change forever.

Epilogue

I'm driving along in my Porsche. I didn't get it by using my wish, of course. This one I earned.

I wrote this story about five years ago. But I was afraid of telling anybody about it. You know, I didn't want anybody to think I was crazy or something. Now that I'm earning my way, I feel a little more confident in talking about my meetings with my genie, Darrell.

You see, I'm doing pretty good right now. Well, a lot better than pretty good. Really good. Really, really good. The oil changes, lube jobs and tune-ups worked like magic. In fact, it's gotten to the point where I can hardly wait for the next ninety days to see what three things I'm going to improve or initiate.

I've got my own real estate company now. The main office is in Portland, Oregon. I've got seventeen branch offices in four states. One of those branch offices is in Maui, Hawaii. That's where I am now. I'm dictating this while I drive from my office to meet my wife at a beautiful seaside restaurant near our beachfront home. Same wife. Terrific woman. It seems that whatever speed bumps we were encountering, we've smoothed them down in ninety-day increments.

As you can guess, my wish—*I wish for success in what I do for a living*—came true. Sure, the wish was the easy part. The harder part was the thinking involved in the *Quarterly Preview*. And it wasn't always easy doing the oil changes, lube jobs and tune-ups. But, as Darrell said, *improvement begets improvement, initiating new things begets initiating new things*. Right from the start, I could feel joy and passion in my job, a job that before I met Darrell I had hated.

Once I started my own business, I took the principles of what I learned from Darrell, Mack, Monica and George and introduced them to my first employee. She loved it! I had hired her as a secretary/receptionist; she is now the chief operating officer. I applied those same principles to my second employee. He loved it. He's now president of our Hawaii operations.

Since it worked so well with me, and then with my first two employees, we decided to make E-W-E a standard with any new employee. The way I look at it is that if each employee improves a little bit in every ninety-day period, our company will grow in geometric dimension.

As I drive to meet my wife at our favorite beachfront restaurant, I notice another Mack's Diner. I stop there almost every day when I'm on Maui. This is the second one on Maui alone. You might have read in *The Wall Street Journal* that he took his company public. I, of course, bought a nice chunk of the initial stock. How could I pass that up? He instilled that same joy and passion in his employees. The stock was a smash hit, making Mack worth over fifty million dollars.

Monica, of course, was instrumental in taking Mack's company public. As George had predicted, she's "running the joint" now. She's president and CEO of one of the largest broker-age firms on Wall Street. In one year, she scored a 'hat trick'—she made the covers of *Business Week, Forbes* and *Fortune*. I see her about once a year. She's having so much fun.

I see George all the time at the airport. Besides some of his regular Japanese travelers, other travelers like me actually wait in line for George. He loves it, of course. Other airlines found out about him and have tried to woo him away with key management positions where he could make a lot more money, but he has turned them all down. He could've taken his airline's early retirement program, but he told me that he was having too much fun doing what he does for a living. This weekend, George and his wife are taking a vacation in Maui. We'll be playing golf on Saturday.

As for Darrell, you're probably not the one that walked up to a soda machine at a gas station and wound up with that big, wonderful genie. After all, what're the odds that it would have been you? A million to one? Five million to one?

No telling where Darrell can be found now. I see him from time to time, but you never know just when he's going to show up. So, if you'd like to have one wish granted, I've got an idea for you that you might be interested in, instead of driving to a lot of gas stations and buying diet colas and pulling tabs all over the place. Darrell appointed me as his surrogate.

Being a 'surrogate genie' is pretty easy for me. I don't even have to eat four cheese-burgers at a time or walk through mirrors. I just have to tell you one thing.

That one thing is to read the sentence I tell you to read out loud.

But, before I will grant you your wish, *you* have to do just one thing. And, you have to do it before you close this book. If you do this one thing, your wish will automatically come true—like Darrell said, *automatically, positively, every time, for everybody.*

That one thing that you have to do is to make a commitment right now to provide the 'oil changes, tune-ups and lube jobs.' This commitment has to be made right now, not tomorrow, not next week.

Your commitment starts by checking one of the boxes on the next page *right now.*

❏ **I'm going to act now.** I'm going to write something in the spaces you provided for my oil changes, tune-ups and lube jobs before I close this book. (If you check this box, your wish will come true.)

❏ **I'm going to procrastinate.** I'm going to write something in those spaces another time. (If you check this box, you significantly increase the degree of difficulty of having your wish come true. Don't let this happen! If you did check this box, erase the check mark. Check the box above. Right now! Believe me, it's so much more fun.)

If you still checked the "I'm going to procrastinate" box, you shouldn't go forward.

You don't often get a second chance with a lot of things in life, but here's a second chance for you to make the commitment that will change your life.

❏ **OK, I'm going to act now.** I'm going to write something in the spaces you provided for my 'oil changes, tune-ups and lube jobs' before I close this book.

Let's proceed.

Read the following sentence out loud: *I wish for success in what I do for a living.*

Go ahead, say it *out loud.*

I grant you your wish.

That's right, your wish has been granted. You'll receive success in whatever you do for a living. That's done. Sorry, I'm not into special effects either.

I'm not going to dictate what your oil changes, lube jobs and tune-ups should be. That is up to you.

Make a list of up to three things you want to improve or initiate over the next ninety days.

Go ahead, think about it for a minute or two and write at least one of them down right now. Remember, you checked the "I'm going to act now" box. So, pal, do it *now.*

1. _____

2. _____

3. _____

To help you with the *one-wish success secret*, I have included a Quarterly Preview Planner in the following pages. There's also a

FREE offer in the back of this book for more. It's easy to use this planner. And it's fun. It will be particularly fun to look back over the years and see all the lube jobs, oil changes and tune-ups that you will have created.

Here's how the Quarterly Preview Planner works:

1. Write down the start date for your first ninety days.
2. Look at a calendar and write down the end date of your first ninety days.
3. Write down up to three things you would like to initiate or improve. A short description is fine—it doesn't have to be lengthy or detailed.
4. Write down some benchmark or measurement for what you want to initiate or improve. Don't worry about setting this benchmark too high or low. Just write something.

Before you go on, I want you to do one last thing for me.

Mark this moment in the margin on this page. Go ahead, write today's date and time.

This could be the start of a real change in your life—an experience whose impact will be felt for many years to come. You'll find that this date will become important to you.

Now that you have written down at least one thing to initiate or improve, you are going to find that those things are going to gnaw at you. It's going to get under your skin. You're going to do something about it. You're going to be taking some very important steps in having your wish come true—to be successful in what you do for a living.

That's it. You're now on your way. Go for it.

You sure are going to have some fun.

1   **Quarterly Preview Planner**

Your First Lube Job, Tune-up, Oil Change

Start date: Day _____ Date _____
90 days later: Day _____ Date _____

	Description	Benchmark
1.		
2.		
3.		

❏ Lube job   ❏ Tune-up   ❏ Oil change

② Quarterly Preview Planner

Your Second Lube Job, Tune-up, Oil Change

Start date: Day _____ Date _____
90 days later: Day _____ Date _____

	Description	Benchmark
1.		
2.		
3.		

❏ Lube job   ❏ Tune-up   ❏ Oil change

3 **Quarterly Preview Planner**

Your Third Lube Job, Tune-up, Oil Change

Start date: Day _____ Date _____

90 days later: Day _____ Date _____

	Description	Benchmark
1.		
2.		
3.		

❑ Lube job   ❑ Tune-up   ❑ Oil change

4 Quarterly Preview Planner

Your Fourth Lube Job, Tune-up, Oil Change

Start date: Day _____ Date _____
90 days later: Day _____ Date _____

	Description	Benchmark
1.		
2.		
3.		

❏ Lube job   ❏ Tune-up   ❏ Oil change

Afterword

Years ago I was thumbing through a magazine in some lobby waiting for a meeting. I read that centuries and centuries ago *opportunity* used to be pictured as a horse. A horse with *wings*. It's not one of those horses that is trained and kneels down. This horse is always moving, flying past you.

I thought about that. If you grab the horse's wings as it approaches, you have a pretty good chance to get a firm grip. Once the horse passes by, however, there is nothing to grab except the tail and that's too slippery.

The Horse of Opportunity could represent a person or a certain job or money or even peace of mind. But many people don't even see the horse coming. Or, they don't reach out early enough to grab the wings. Or, they are afraid to grab on not knowing where the Horse of Opportunity will take them. Most of my life, I've been fortunate and have seen the horse coming and have been able to get a firm grip on the wings. The horse has carried me to some terrific "destinations." I've had wonderful, wonderful rides on that Horse of Opportunity.

Now I see that horse coming right at *you*.

How can I see that with you being where you are and me being here? Well, because you are reading this. I'm assuming you have just read *Success Is Just One Wish Away*. By reading this book, you've stirred up that horse. The Horse of Opportunity is indeed heading in your direction!

At first, it may seem difficult to grab on to the wings of a flying horse. Not so. Here's why. First of all, you see the horse coming. By seeing the horse, you can *prepare* to grab the wings. If you prepare, all you have to do is *grab* the wings when the Horse of Opportunity gallops by. How do you prepare? Pretty easy. Think of up to three things that you would like to improve or initiate and write them down in the spaces in the first

Quarterly Preview. Just write them down. The rest will take care of itself.

If you haven't done that, do it now. And then get ready for the ride of your life on the Horse of Opportunity.

Order Form

Order more books for friends and loved ones, for somebody you'd like to inspire or even whose life you want to influence for the better. Or even just to have and pass out to anybody you feel could benefit from the important message in this book. Simply fill out the order form and we'll be happy to ship one or several copies to you or to those on your mailing list. (Your name will appear on the mailing label as the giver of this gift.)

❑ Please send me _____ copies of your book, *Success Is Just One Wish Away* @ $19.95 each.

❑ Please send me FREE Quarterly Preview Planner cards. I am enclosing a business-sized self-addressed stamped envelope.

❑ Please send one book to each name and address on the list enclosed.

❑ Enclosed is my check for $ _____

❑ Please charge my credit card number:

_____ Exp.: _____

We accept Visa, MasterCard, and American Express.

Signature _____

❑ Please ship to:

Name _____
Address_____
City_____ State____ Zip_____
Daytime Phone: _____

(continued on next page)

Postage and Handling

$4 per order postage and handling for regular shipping. Add $3 per book for Priority Mail shipments. Add $10 for FedEx shipments. Lower shipping and handling costs for bulk orders.

Schools and Businesses:

Quantity discounts are available for schools and businesses that order 3 books or more. The following schedule applies:

3 to 199 . . . . 20% off $15.95 ea.
200 to 499. . . . . . 30% off $13.95 ea.
500 or more . . . . 40% off $11.95 ea.

Call toll-free (800) 323-6400
Fax your order (702) 597-2002

Mail orders to:

> Delstar Books
>
> Department   **0170**
>
> 3350 Palms Center Drive
>
> Las Vegas, NV 89103